Studies on Ethnic Groups in China

STEVAN HARRELL, Editor

HENRY M. JACKSON SCHOOL OF INTERNATIONAL STUDIES
Studies on Ethnic Groups in China

Cultural Encounters on China's Ethnic Frontiers
Edited by Stevan Harrell

Guest People: Hakka Identity in China and Abroad
Edited by Nicole Constable

Familiar Strangers: A History of Muslims in Northwest China
Jonathan N. Lipman

*Lessons in Being Chinese: Minority Education
and Ethnic Identity in Southwest China*
Mette Halskov Hansen

*Manchus and Han: Ethnic Relations and Political Power
in Late Qing and Early Republican China, 1861–1928*
Edward J. M. Rhoads

Ways of Being Ethnic in Southwest China
Stevan Harrell

Governing China's Multiethnic Frontiers
Edited by Morris Rossabi

*On the Margins of Tibet:
Cultural Survival on the Sino-Tibetan Frontier*
Åshild Kolås and Monika Thowsen

The Art of Ethnography: A Chinese "Miao Album"
Translation by David M. Deal and Laura Hostetler

The Art of Ethnography

A Chinese "Miao Album"

Translation by

DAVID M. DEAL and LAURA HOSTETLER

Introduction by

LAURA HOSTETLER

UNIVERSITY OF WASHINGTON PRESS

Seattle & London

The Art of Ethnography was published with the assistance
of the Getty Grant Program.
Additional support was provided by Whitman College.

University of Washington Press
P.O. Box 50096, Seattle, WA 98145
www.washington.edu/uwpress

Library of Congress Cataloging-in-Publication Data

The art of ethnography : a Chinese "Miao album" / translation
by David Deal and Laura Hostetler.—1st ed.
p.   cm. —(Studies on ethnic groups in China)
Translation of anonymous and untitled Chinese work,
dating from some time after 1797.
Includes bibliographical references and index.
ISBN 0-295-98543-7 (hardback : alk. paper)
1. Minorities—China—Guizhou Sheng.   2. Guizhou Sheng (China)—
Ethnic relations.   I. Title: Chinese "Miao album".   II. Deal, David
Michael, 1939–   III. Hostetler, Laura.   IV. Series.
DS793.K8A77   2005
305.895'97205134—dc22   2005024390

For Judy,

and the generosity of her love — D.M.D.

For John A. Hostetler,

who loved beautiful books,

and

Beulah S. Hostetler,

faithful editor, author, and guide — L.H.

Contents

Preface

QING dynasty "Miao albums" are of interest to scholars not only for their valuable ethnohistorical information concerning the local peoples of southwest China, but also for the insights they provide into the ambivalent views of these "barbarians" held by members of the Chinese gentry class, by and for whom the albums were produced. The album presented here is a fine example of the genre, its detailed illustrations and balanced calligraphy revealing the reason why the albums have been so cherished by collectors.

While on sabbatical leave at Harvard University in 1976–77, David Deal received a photocopy of this album from someone at the Freer Gallery of Art and Arthur M. Sackler Gallery at the Smithsonian Institution, together with a letter asking if he knew what it was. While the name of the sender is no longer known, it is not surprising that she or he would have singled out David, for at the time he was one of only a handful of American scholars researching the history of ethnic minorities in southwest China. Although the "opening" of China to foreign researchers in the last three decades has prompted many more American scholars to develop an interest in southwestern minorities, none perhaps is so qualified to work on this project as Laura Hostetler. Professor Hostetler's research on Miao albums (published in 2001) led David to seek her out as a collaborator about a year before his death. The Introduction to this book reflects her deep knowledge of the subject, while the final translations owe a great deal to her poetic sensitivity to the originals.

A few months before David Deal died in October 2001, he asked me if I would write this preface. As his student, colleague, and friend, I am honored to do so.

David's interest in southwest China developed during his graduate school years at the University of Washington, where he studied Chinese history under Jack Dull, and was stimulated by the University's strong Tibetan Studies program. His doctoral thesis, "National Minority Policy in Southwest China, 1911–1965" (University of Washington, 1971), focuses on the continuities and differences between Republican and early-Communist-era minority policies. Written as a political history, it is at the same time deeply anthropological; this quality characterized David's research and teaching throughout his life. When I took his classes in modern Chinese history at Whitman College in the 1970s, a significant number of our readings were by anthropologists focusing on the peoples of western China. While studies of ethnicity in late-imperial and modern China are now fashionable in American sinological circles, at that time there were very few "modern China" courses that looked anything like David's.

David is remembered as a dedicated teacher, a sensitive and capable administrator, and a dedicated advocate for Asian Studies at Whitman College. When he arrived at the College in 1969, he was the only person who taught anything related to Asia, and his six core courses—traditional and modern sections of Japanese, Chinese, and Indian histories —would certainly be considered an outrageous stretch by today's standards. Beginning in the mid-1970s he lobbied hard for Asian Studies at Whitman, and over the next two decades new faculty positions were added in Chinese and Japanese languages and literature, in the anthropology of Asia, in South Asian religion, in South Asian politics, and most recently in East Asian art history. In 1994 these efforts gave rise to the creation of an Asian Studies major, from which we now graduate about eight to ten students per year.

In 1979, when David led a dozen wheat farmers from Walla Walla on an agricultural tour of China, he met with faculty and administrators at several Chinese universities and discussed the possibility of creating an exchange program. Upon the group's return, financial gifts were made to the College by several tour participants, among others, to support the development of such a program. A large gift from one of the College's great benefactors, Donald Sherwood, allowed the establishment of the Whitman-in-China program in 1982. I was fortunate to be one of the first candidates selected for that program, which is now in its twenty-second year. Every year we send four to six Whitman alumni (usually recent graduates) to teach English in three Chinese universities, and we invite two or three young Chinese faculty from those same schools to study as Sherwood Scholars at Whitman. Over the years, more than a hundred Whitman alumni have had the opportunity to teach in China, and more than forty Chinese scholars have studied at Whitman.

In alternate summers, the College also runs an intensive Chinese language program at Yunnan University for Whitman students. All of the participants in this program receive scholarships amounting to about half of their expenses from the David Deal–China Exchange Endowment, which was created in 2000 through a large gift from an anonymous donor. In 2001, former Chinese and American participants in the Whitman-in-China program joined together to establish the David M. Deal Scholarship to provide financial aid for Chinese students studying at Whitman.

David's devotion to teaching and to administering the College, including eight years as Dean of Faculty, did not allow time for him to finish the two book manuscripts he was working on at the time of his death. The completion of this book was particularly important to him in his last days, and he wanted to thank a number of people for their help. In addition to his collaborator, Laura Hostetler, he was particularly grateful to Burton Pu, for help with the original translations of the poems and prose, beginning in 1985; former student Zhou Minfang, and her husband, John Chian, for their help in searching (alas, unsuccessfully) for the original album manuscript; Lorri Hagman at the University of Washington Press, for keeping the project together over the past three years; Stevan Harrell, editor of this series, for promoting the manuscript and helping David to connect with Lorri and Laura; Milo Beach and Linda Machado at the Smithsonian Institution's Freer Gallery of Art and Arthur M. Sackler Gallery for their help in locating and reproducing the photographic plates that are the only copy of the manuscript upon which this book is based; Robbie Skiles, for typing the original manuscript; and the Aid to Scholarly and Instructional Development Fund, the Faculty Scholarship Reserve Fund, and the Department of History, all at Whitman College, for financial support in the production of this book.

My personal debt to David is beyond measure. I thanked him when he was alive, but I will do it again here. I think that my job—researching, writing, and teaching about the peoples of southwest China—is just about the most interesting, rewarding, and enjoyable thing I could ever hope to do. And it all goes back to the spring of 1976: Freshman Seminar no. 16–Chinese Social Institutions, with Professor David M. Deal. I got a "B" in the course. Thanks, Dave.

CHARLES F. McKHANN
Walla Walla, Washington, October 2005

Acknowledgments

ALTHOUGH this work was co-authored, writing the acknowledgments fell to me when David Deal passed away in the autumn of 2001, a few months after my own father died. This book is dedicated to David's wife, Judy Deal; to my father, John A. Hostetler, who shared his understanding of ethnic religious groups outside the cultural mainstream with his family and with the world; and to my mother, Beulah S. Hostetler, who read and commented on the entire manuscript but left us to join David and my father when the book was still in proof stage.

I want to express my thanks to Stevan Harrell for bringing David Deal and me together and to David for placing his trust in me as co-author. David had completed a draft translation of the album reproduced here and initiated inquiries at the University of Washington Press before I became involved in the project. Early in 2001, after learning of David's failing health, I offered to work with him as joint author. We agreed that I would draft an introduction that would set the album in its historical context and go over the translations. As it turned out, David did not have the opportunity to comment on the Introduction, but I did extensively review each translation. We did not meet in person, but carried on a lively e-mail exchange over the course of about six months. More recently, I have envisioned his spirit as a gentle presence when working on this project, encouraging me to persevere.

In refining the translations, my goals were to reflect as closely as possible the original content of the Chinese, while striving for clarity and fluidity in English. My guiding principle was shaped by three readers. The first was avidly interested in ethnographic content for scholarly purposes but not trained to read the original Chinese. This reader helped me be as faithful as possible to the original text. The second had more general interest in the content, but knew relatively little about the Chinese context or ethnology per se. Her job was to keep me from straying into esoterica and to remind me to provide notes to explain the allusions found in the original text. The third was a specialist in Chinese ethnic minorities able to critique both my translations and interpretations. The comments of all were invaluable.

The most extensive alterations I made to David's translation were to the poetry. The Chinese poems found in the album are each comprised of four lines of seven characters. Whereas David's translations were free form, the final translations that appear here reflect the regularity of the meter, but with a different rhythm: four lines of twelve syllables each. I made no attempt at rhyming. When translating the poetry I was guided by the same standards I applied to the prose text. However, I sometimes opted to retain fidelity to general imagery or the spirit of the poem rather than adhere to a literal translation. Readers will find that such editorial choices are described in the notes.

My heartfelt thanks go to Lorri Hagman at the University of Washington Press and to Chas McKhann, David's colleague at Whitman College, for their tremendous support in a complicated collaborative project of a truly interdisciplinary nature, and for their patience when I found myself having to push back deadlines. Careful readings and detailed comments from Press readers Stevan Harrell and Louisa Schein helped me to better engage in dialogue with the discipline of anthropology. I am grateful to the Getty Foundation for a grant making possible the inclusion of color plates and to the University of Washington Press for pursuing that grant. The Institute for Humanities and the Office of the Vice Chancellor for Research at the University of Illinois at Chicago provided funding for research at the Società Geografica Italiana in Rome and the Bibliothèque nationale in Paris, as well as assistance with expenses related to reproduction and permission fees for photography. Whitman College also provided assistance with expenses related to photography. The Smithsonian Institution, Società Geografica Italiana, British Library, Bibliothèque nationale de France, and University of Pennsylvania Museum allowed me to reproduce works in their collections. Victor Mair kindly addressed questions related to a number of complexities in the translations. Stevan Harrell also graciously lent his own linguistic and ethnographic expertise to a final review of the translations, for which I am, again, most grateful. Final decisions were my own, and I take responsibility for them as well as for any errors or inconsistencies that may have crept into the manuscript.

Finally, I thank my families, both extended and immediate, for their tangible and their intangible support over the course of this project.

LAURA HOSTETLER
Oak Park, IL

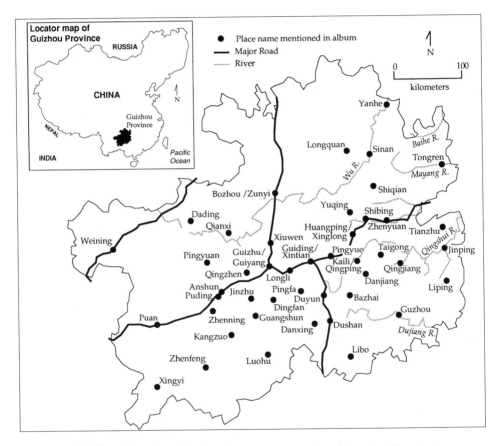

Guizhou circa 1820, showing place names mentioned in the album texts. Cartography Laboratory, Department of Anthropology, University of Illinois at Chicago.

Introduction:
Early Modern Ethnography
in Comparative Historical Perspective

LAURA HOSTETLER

FROM costume books to portrayals of "exotic" peoples in distant lands, ethnographic interest in the "Other" has often been associated with European colonial projects.[1] Yet, ethnographic representation was practiced by expanding powers in many parts of the world, not only by European or "Western" states. During the eighteenth century, Qing China (1636–1911) saw an increase in the literary and artistic representation of different peoples, including the rise of a systematic ethnography of ethnic minority groups.[2] In 1751 the Qianlong emperor commissioned the *Qing Imperial Illustrations of Tributary Peoples* (Huang Qing zhigong tu). The work is an illustrated compilation describing peoples from around the world, including the frontier areas of China proper, the far reaches of the Qing empire, and foreign countries (encompassing various parts of Europe).[3] The most elaborate edition is a set of scrolls containing 304 color paintings on silk with accompanying descriptive text in both Chinese and Manchu (see pls. 1 and 2).[4] The illustrations depict a wide variety of peoples in colorful and distinctive costumes. The text describes where the peoples represented lived, their relationship to the Qing empire, and any distinctive customs for which they were known.

The section of *Illustrations of Tributary Peoples* that describes the culturally non-Chinese peoples[5] of southwest China may well have been based on a genre of illustrated manuscripts known in English as "Miao albums" (*Miaoman tu* or *Bai Miao tu* in Chinese). The earliest of these albums were compiled by officials responsible for governing frontier areas during the late Yongzheng (r. 1723–35) or early Qianlong (r. 1736–96) periods. The texts of the Miao albums and *Illustrations of Tributary Peoples* are not identical, nor is the layout of the illustrations the same; yet in their overall design and even in specific aspects of their content they exhibit striking similarities.

Plate 1. Foreigners from "Heleweicaiya." Huang Qing zhigong tu. *National Palace Museum, Taipei, Taiwan, Republic of China.*

Plate 2. (Kayou) Zhongjia. Huang Qing zhigong tu. *National Palace Museum, Taipei, Taiwan, Republic of China.*

The *Illustrations of Tributary Peoples* showcases pairs of male and female figures in distinctive costumes, often shown together with an artifact that evokes a characteristic cultural practice. For example, a colorful ball made of ribbon is suspended between a couple representing one of Guizhou's ethnic minority groups, the Kayou Zhongjia (pl. 2). The scene portrays a courtship custom in which lovers tossed a ball back and forth to signal their mutual affection. No background scenery is shown for the focus is on the peoples themselves, not so much on the locales in which they dwelled. The goal of the compendium was to demonstrate the multiplicity of peoples united in their recognition of Qing sovereignty. The commissioning edict clearly described this: "My dynasty has united the vast expanses. Of all the inner and outer barbarians belonging under its jurisdiction, there are none that have not sincerely turned toward Us and been transformed."[6] The completed work was to serve as a testament to the glory and achievements of the Qing, and specifically the Qianlong emperor's reign.

The illustrations in the Miao albums, on the other hand, are less formal and more rustic.[7] Larger groups of people, young and old, are depicted in a natural setting. Quite often they are engaged in the same cultural activity that the *Illustrations of Tributary Peoples* alludes to through the presence of a signifying cultural object. For example, the illustration of the Kayou Zhongjia in the album reproduced below (fig. 6) shows six individuals frolicking outside with their partners on a spring day. Here, too, the colorful balls serve as a trope that identifies the group. The background scenery reflects variations in topography, level of architectural sophistication, and other features of the environment that may have held significance for the album's readership. Whereas a given group's preference for living next to water, in the mountains, or near a market town where individuals could sell their handiwork was of little direct importance to the emperor, this level of detail would have mattered to local officials. Although the specifics of design and specialized function distinguish the Miao albums from the *Illustrations of Tributary Peoples*, both genres attest to the existence of a detailed and highly complex taxonomy of ethnically diverse peoples that was part and parcel of the Qing state's immensely successful efforts at empire building.[8]

What distinguishes these works as "ethnographic" is their purported basis in direct observation. Many of the earlier written descriptions about

China's Others, such as the *Classic of Mountains and Seas* (Shanhai jing) and a Ming (1368–1644) encyclopaedia known as the *San cai tu hui*, relied heavily, and sometimes exclusively, on earlier textual descriptions.[9] The preface to at least one edition of the *Qing Imperial Illustrations of Tributary Peoples* specifically claims that those produced under the Qianlong emperor were more reliable and true to life than *Illustrations of Tributary Peoples* produced under earlier dynasties.[10] The archival record bears out this claim. An edict received by the governor-general of Sichuan in 1750, prior to the formal commissioning of the project, directed him to "take the western barbarians, and the Luoluo with which you are familiar, and make illustrations and commentary concerning the appearance of the men and women, their dress, ornamentation, clothing, and customs." It also specifically stated that at this time he should not send anyone to make inquiries about those with whom he had no familiarity.[11] Judging by the context, the emperor wanted only information grounded in personal experience. The edict implies that documentation of other, more remote, groups should await further instruction.

The actual commissioning edict, which shortly followed that received by the Sichuan governor-general, specified how the groundwork for the *Illustrations of Tributary Peoples* was to be carried out:

> As for their clothing, caps, appearance, and bearing, each has its differences. Now although we have likenesses from several places, they are not yet uniform and complete. Gather together the several models that we now have, and deliver them to each of the governors and governors-general near the borders. Order them to take the Miao, Yao, Li, and Zhuang under their jurisdiction, as well as the various outer barbarians, and according to these examples copy their appearance, bearing, clothing and ornaments; make illustrations and send them to the Grand Council for classification and arrangement for presentation and inspection [by the emperor].[12]

The edict specifically described the procedures that should be followed in completing the work. Models based on likenesses of peoples that had already been submitted from a number of border areas were to be transmitted to the governors and governors-general in areas from which no illustrations had yet been forthcoming. Images were to be made according to these models, that is, following the form, but with relevant local content. The sum total would then be sent to the capital, where they would be arranged into a format worthy of the emperor's inspection. The completed work would allow him to survey his empire, his subjects, and his accomplishments, and also to leave a record of them for posterity. The *Illustrations of Tributary Peoples* was to serve as a reflection of the order the empire had helped to create. At the same time, it served to justify and to perpetuate the type of relationships the Qing enjoyed with its tributaries.

We have less direct information about the origins of the Miao albums, but do know from several extant prefaces that at least some of them were made by lower-level officials posted to frontier regions. These individuals based their work on a combination of firsthand experience and research into accounts of customs recorded in local gazetteers of the province. In the only case where the identity of the artist is mentioned, he is said to have been a long-time resident of the area who had a thorough familiarity with his subject matter.[13] It is possible that the early Miao albums may have served as drafts for the *Illustrations of Tributary Peoples*.[14] The album texts were largely based on information in local gazetteers, which were regularly revised and expanded from around 1600 through 1750 on what appears to have been the basis of direct observation. As in the case of the *Illustrations of Tributary Peoples*, this rootedness in observation (however imperfect) is what makes the albums "ethnographic," and is also what allows us to understand them as part of an early modern phenomenon also seen outside of China.

This book contains the complete reproduction of a Miao album with a fully annotated translation into English. The album reproduced here is, like most, anonymous and untitled. Dating from sometime after 1797, it is neither one of the earliest nor one of the latest examples, and is typical of the genre at the height of its distribution when albums were routinely hand-copied from existing models.[15] This album identifies eighty-two different ethnic groups residing in Guizhou.[16] A separate hand-painted illustration, textual description, and poem is devoted to each ethnic group.[17] The multifaceted nature of the work makes it of value to ethnographers, art historians, and historians of China, as well as those interested in the cultural side of early modern imperial expansion from a comparative angle.

This introductory essay situates these examples of early modern Chinese ethnography within two different contexts. By locating the development of the albums within the Qing empire, we can trace the genesis of the genre and the sociopolitical context in which the albums were first made; lay out what is known of the albums' authorship and their production; explore the basis for the composition of the illustrations; discuss the ethnographic content of the texts; and finally, trace the evolution of the genre over time. In addition, situating the production of these Miao albums and related *Illustrations of Tributary Peoples* within the broader early modern context of imperial expansion permits a broader historical analysis through a comparison of these ethnographic documents with other roughly contemporaneous ethnographic depictions from Tokugawa Japan and the Ottoman empire.[18] The goal is to show that during the early modern period, defined roughly as 1500–1800, a variety of different expanding states and empires gathered and recorded information about peoples with whom they were coming into contact, whether through exploration, direct colonization, or diplomacy. Ethnographic interest in other peoples was not simply a "Western" phenomenon, but rather was part of a much more widespread process of state building in that period. This assessment is an effort to make visible some of the similarities shared by early modern states in their attempts to categorize, represent, and ultimately, to construct knowledge about peoples from other ethnic and cultural backgrounds.[19]

MIAO ALBUMS

The region we now call southwest China was only loosely integrated into the Qing empire during the early eighteenth century. The area had long served as a buffer zone between dynastic China and the countries beyond. Since the early Ming (1368–1644), native chiefs (*tusi*) had been recognized by the throne and therefore ruled the area by proxy. By virtue of their inherited position, the *tusi* enjoyed great autonomy, governing as they saw fit. Gradually, however, their power was eroded as regions that had been under their jurisdiction were transferred to direct administrative rule by officials in the imperial bureaucracy. This process, known in Chinese as *gaitu guiliu*, intensified under the Qing, most dramatically through the militarily aggressive policies of the Yongzheng emperor.[20] The changes in governance he instituted not only had implications for legal procedures and taxation, but even restricted the expression of cultural activities such as gatherings on

festival days and regulated the types of dress that were to be permitted.[21] Confucian-trained scholar officials from other parts of the empire
would now be assigned to govern these remote frontier regions. The
Miao albums served an important purpose by providing the new
officials with information about the populations to be governed.

Miao albums are bound collections of hand-painted color illustrations of ethnic minority groups paired with hand-written annotations
in classical Chinese. Because most Miao albums are anonymous and
undated, the emergence of the genre is difficult to trace with precision.
We do know, however, that they first appeared toward the end of the
Yongzheng reign during the implementation of *gaitu guiliu*, or during the early years of the Qianlong emperor's reign in the aftermath
of widespread rebellion against its repressive policies. The prose texts
of the albums were derived from portions of local gazetteers describing the customs (*fengsu*) of non-Chinese inhabitants of the province.
Local artists painted the illustrations that were sometimes later recopied
by artists who had less, if any, familiarity with their subject matter.
Together, the texts and illustrations record information on the provenance, whereabouts, character, beliefs, and cultural practices of the
broad range of groups that the albums identify. The dominant
Confucian values of Chinese society that emphasized the proper performance of ritual—particularly in the areas of marriage and funeral
practices, but also through norms for diet, dress, and the observance
of annual festivals—undoubtedly shaped the categories of inquiry. The
albums also show an interest in the means of livelihood of the various
groups discussed, as well as in their "natures." Overall, these documents give witness to the state's desire to know, as well as to control,
its southern frontier territories and peoples. Miao albums exist for various parts of south and southwest China, including Guizhou, Yunnan,
Guangdong, Hunan, Taiwan, and Hainan.[22] While all of these albums
show great similarity in both design and general content, the albums
for Guizhou have been studied most extensively.[23]

The albums portray not only Miao peoples strictly speaking, but also
other *miaoman*, or non-Han ethnic groups. In classical Chinese, Miao
has two usages relevant to our purposes here. Both are used in the
albums. The looser usage, reflected in the variety of titles under which
the albums circulated, refers broadly to non-Han peoples in south and
southwest China. Hence the somewhat misleading label "Miao album."

The other meaning of the term Miao was circumscribed more narrowly, as is the normal usage of "Miao" in English. It referred specifically to the Miao ethnic minority who are distinguished in the Guizhou album reproduced here from other minority groups such as the Gelao, Zhuang, Zhongjia, Luoluo, Yao, Dong, and others.

Today, "Miao" is a highly contested term with a variety of usages. In the People's Republic of China, "the Miao" are one of fifty-five nationally recognized ethnic minority groups (*minzu*).[24] Many English speakers use the term Miao to refer to members of this same ethnic group who migrated from China into Southeast Asia and later, in the aftermath of the Vietnam war, to the United States.[25] Most "Miao" living outside China do not, however, self-identify as Miao but rather as Hmong. Miao is, after all, not an indigenous word, but a Chinese ethnonym, although it is probably the Chinese transliteration of the native word for Hmong.[26] To further complicate matters, the correlation between those groups who were called Miao in the albums and those who bear that name within China today is not necessarily entirely consistent.

The term Han also begs a word of explanation. The word itself is ancient, but like many words has undergone substantial shifts in meaning and usage over time. The Chinese character for the Han majority ethnic group is the same as that for the Han dynasty, which ruled China from 206 B.C.E. to 220 C.E. In the Miao albums, the word Han was used to differentiate what we would now call culturally Chinese peoples from those with different ethnic and cultural backgrounds. During the early twentieth century, the term Han became associated with Chinese ethnic nationalism under the political leadership of Sun Yat-sen, who used it as a banner to unite the Chinese people in opposition to the Manchu ruling house.[27] Today, although Han denotes the majority ethnic group in China, it also carries political overtones different from its eighteenth-century usage. I use "Han" below as it is used in the albums to describe a cultural norm against which the ethnic Others in the albums are implicitly, and sometimes explicitly, described.

The term Chinese also commonly carries at least two layers of meaning. In popular usage it is more or less synonymous with "Han." "Chinese" also refers to citizens of China—of whatever ethnic origin.[28] I use "Chinese" here to describe the more or less coherent dominant culture largely shaped by and conveyed through the Chinese written language. I prefer not to use "Han"—except when, and as, it is used in the albums—so as not to inadvertently invoke meanings that were not part of its eighteenth-century usage.

Album Illustrations

The album as a venue for artwork in China dates from at least as early as the Song dynasty (960–1278), when bird and flower painting came into vogue.[29] Landscape paintings accompanied by poetry also appeared in albums. The Miao albums, however, seem more closely related to albums that had a more ideological or instructive purpose such as *Illustrations of Weaving and Tilling* (Gengzhi tu), which first appeared during the Song dynasty, but were later reissued during the Qing;[30] or illustrated manuals that described a complex series of steps in porcelain manufacture.[31] The Miao albums, rather than serving primarily as a repository for art—whether visual or literary—constituted instead a kind of practical map for locating different groups in space, and for codifying or predicting their behavior. They were, among other things, an effort to describe and to better understand the natural world and its inhabitants. It is no coincidence that Miao albums emerged at roughly the same time that travel writing became more prevalent in China. A number of albums actually include topographical maps.[32]

The illustrations and texts are components of equal importance in the Miao albums.[33] Like the texts, discussed in more detail below, the illustrations drew their inspiration and models in part from local gazetteers. For Guizhou, the earliest visual representations we have of native peoples are found in the 1673 and 1692 editions of the *Guizhou Gazetteer* (Guizhou tongzhi). These works contain thirty and thirty-one wood block illustrations respectively. In terms of composition, the illustrations in the 1692 gazetteer bear a resemblance to the later hand-painted Miao albums that normally include visual and textual depictions of eighty-two groups. These eighty-two standard images, once established, were repeated with some variations across the albums of Guizhou. The illustrations, in a sense, go further than the texts by providing the viewer with a single mental image or template of each different ethnic group. The texts by contrast describe a variety of characteristics, thus providing a somewhat more multifaceted view. Repeated across the albums, that same image becomes the defining feature, or trope, for that group. Thus, for example, the Mulao are shown sacrificing a chicken, and preparing a straw dragon with flags, each of a different color, sticking into its back (fig. 30). The Black Luoluo (fig. 1) are on horseback returning from a hunt. The Red Miao fight amongst themselves, with the women restraining their menfolk (fig. 14). The Gou'er Longjia dance outside around a tall pole (fig. 10). In this way, each of the identified groups becomes strongly associated with the primary characteristic depicted in the illustration accompanying the somewhat more nuanced ethnographic text.[34] As with the texts, there can be some variation in detail from album to album, but the general themes and composition remain largely the same. For each group pictured, not only is the same visual trope repeated across the albums but the figures often occupy the same position on the page.

Lothar Ledderose has proposed that in Chinese culture, art—from language, to architecture, to the plastic and visual arts, and even to food preparation—is produced through the recombination of units, which he calls modules. Most relevant for our purposes here is his discussion of the various versions of the "Ten Kings of Hell" paintings dating from the thirteenth century.[35] He shows that such paintings were produced in sets, and that while there was some room for variation from set to set, certain features—especially the position and number of figures in a given scene—tend to remain constant. From this he concludes that the artists probably used stencils to give them "a firm compositional framework in which to operate."[36] Furthermore, several artists may also have worked on different aspects of the same paintings. With certain features of the painting already formulated, and one's work niche narrowly carved out, original creative work was limited in this context to such areas as designing the patterns depicted on clothing or fabric.[37] Most of the Miao albums appear to have been made by paid artists in a workshop setting where the overall composition of the illustrations was largely predetermined.

As alluded to above, the names of a number of Guizhou's non-Han minority groups were derived from characteristics of their outward appearance. These included distinctive hairstyles, the color or other aspects of their clothing, identifying behaviors or practices, as well as their dwelling places. These features were often depicted in the illustrations, as highlighted in the selection of color plates. Notice the distinctive hairstyle on the Guoquan (Pot-Ring) Gelao, who are preparing sacrifices to a divinity represented by a tiger's head made out of flour paste (pl. 3). The Louju Hei Miao's distinctive housing arrangements with room for cattle on the ground level of their houses are depicted in plate 4. Plate 5 depicts the Daya (Teeth-Breaking) Gelao engaged in the activity for which they are named. This particular illustration shows an example of an album where the descriptive text appears on the same page as the illustration. It is also one of several albums that does not include background scenery. Nüguan, the first wife of the Luoluo chief, is shown in plate 6. We see her in regal majesty, a woman who may assume rule of her people should her husband die and a son not yet be of age. The illustration of the Hua Gelao reproduced in plate 7 is included here to demonstrate the range of styles found within the Miao album genre.[38] Two figures with primitively depicted features are dressed in colorful outfits. Although we know that the texts have roots in direct observation, there is some question as to the basis for the illustrations. Aside from the one album preface whose author claims to have lived in Guizhou for many years, and to have drawn from his local knowledge in making the illustrations, we do not have evidence that the artists were familiar with their subjects. In cases where they were not simply copying another album they may have taken their inspiration from the names or from the actual costumes and other distinctive visual features of the groups in question.[39]

If, as suggested above, most of the albums were made by paid artists in a workshop setting, it is not surprising that illustrations may have sometimes been reproduced by artists unfamiliar with their subject matter. Under these conditions, odd or exaggerated effects within the parameters permitted by the genre could easily be introduced. Across the albums, the short-skirt Miao are, for example, depicted in skirts of varying lengths, some portrayals being much more titillating than others. The hairstyle of the Madeng (Stirrup) Longjia also shows significant variation.[40] While no two albums are identical, the composition of the illustrations—even down to the placement of individual figures on the page—can be quite similar.[41] Compare, for example, the two illustrations of the Turen in figure 33 and plate 8. There is also evidence that, at least some of the time, the figures as well as the natural scenery and buildings were painted by two different artists as in the paintings of the "Ten Kings of Hell" that Ledderose describes. An apparently unfinished album in the collection of the University Museum at the University of Pennsylvania includes only figures but no background scenery (pl. 9). These figures are nearly identical to those found in an album housed in the British Library that does include background scenery (pl. 10).

While the early albums were originally made to serve a utilitarian function, the genre eventually evolved to fill other niches as well. The lower quality workshop albums may have catered to an audience interested in the exotic, paralleling the demand for armchair ethnographies in Europe. The fact that they are anonymous shows that those who painted them either did not care to, or were not in a position to claim authorship. A higher quality market for the albums also apparently developed simultaneously. In these albums, the identity of the artist and calligrapher is indicated by the presence of seals or sometimes a signature. Such an indication of the author's identity demonstrates evidence of pride in their production (see pls. 4 and 11). In these later albums the artistry may have been valued as much or even more than the ethnographic content they contained. Some albums were penned in a variety of calligraphic styles. Plate 11 shows an opening from an album, the text of which is written in a style evocative of ancient seal script. Other albums were penned by the hand of one or more local notables. The artists of a number of these later albums also took more liberty in terms of the composition of the illustrations, as well as the portrayal of the various groups depicted.

The colorful and "exotic" albums sometimes found their way out of the locality in which they were made when a local official moved on to take up a post in another part of the empire. Miao albums were also circulated when bestowed as gifts on superiors. In such cases, the underlying message from the giver was two-fold. The gift at once communicated both the giver's appreciation of art and fine calligraphy, as well as the diligence and seriousness with which he approached his frontier post.

At any rate, the Miao album was not an insignificant genre. Albums were actively produced for a period of at least 150 years, and in significant numbers for handmade documents; over one hundred eighty albums are extant and housed in various libraries and museums throughout Asia, Europe, and the United States.[42] Others remain in private hands. During the 1860s, a century after they began to be made, the albums started to appear in used bookstores and on the foreign art market in Chinese cities.[43] Purchased by European and American expa-

锅割花桃在平远州属以葛织斜文布
为衣妇人以青布束乱髪如锅圈状辰
青短裙害指病不脈药则延巫师以帚
头一具用五色绒装饰置籏箕曰祷之
嗜酒而惰农业壅则倒置其尸谓使之
不知
来发锅圈倩巫师   驱人绒师兇头箕
醉卿酩酊田成石   欲阻魂归倒置尸圆圈

Plate 3. Guoquan (Pot-Ring) Gelao. Società Geografica Italiana. Chinese Catalog no. 63.

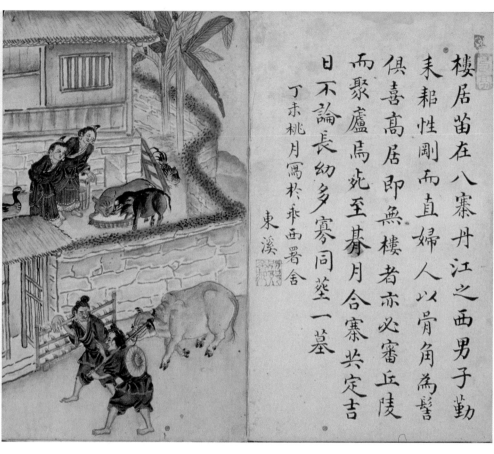

樓居苗在八寨丹江之西男子勤
未耜性剛而直婦人以骨角為簪
俱喜高居即無樓者亦必審丘陵
而聚廬焉死至碁月合寨共定吉
日不論長幼多寡同塋一墓

東溪

丁未桃月寫於粤西署舍

Plate 4. Louju (Storied-Dwelling) Miao. The seal identifies the calligrapher (who
may also have been the artist); the smaller characters indicate the date and the
location where the text was penned. By permission of the British Library, Or 11513.

打牙犵狫在
貴陽各屬獷
悍輕生女將
嫁則打去門
牙以防妨夫
云

Plate 5. Daya (Teeth-Breaking) Gelao. By permission of the British Library, Or 4153.

Plate 6. Nüguan. By permission of the British Library, Add 16594.

花猙老
鋤地

Plate 7. Hua Gelao. From Miaoman tu. This is one of the cruder representations from a Miao album. Courtesy of the Institute of History and Philology, Academia Sinica.

Plate 8. Turen. By permission of the British Library, Add 16594.

Plate 9. Datou Longjia. University of Pennsylvania Museum, neg. P4-2566.

Plate 10. Datou Longjia. By permission of the British Library, Or 13504.

Plate 11. Yangbao Miao. The calligraphy in the album is written in a number of different styles, but the seals indicate that each page was penned by the same hand. Società Geografica Italiana. Chinese Catalog 63.

triates who found them attractive—or at least objects worthy of curios-
ity—they became geographically highly dispersed. Scholars have taken
an interest in the albums for over a century, with the first translations
into European languages already appearing at the end of the nineteenth
century. The earliest scholarship tended to describe a single album and
its contents. Beginning in the 1960s, the genre itself received attention
with questions about authorship, dating, and accuracy starting to take
precedence. Only more recently have the albums been given book-length
treatment, and studied as part of the Qing effort to create and main-
tain a multiethnic empire.[44]

Album Texts

Ethnographic descriptions of culturally non-Chinese peoples in southwest China appeared as early as 1560.[45] Over the course of the next two-
and-a-half centuries, these texts, found both in officially commissioned
local gazetteers and in private writings, came to reflect an expanded
knowledge of the groups they describe and, correspondingly, an increasingly complex taxonomy. In 1608, *A Record of Guizhou Province* (Qian
ji) contained headings for thirteen different groups. Three editions of
the *Guizhou Gazetteer* dating from 1673, 1692, and 1741 contained thirty,
thirty-one, and thirty-eight groups respectively. An 1834 publication also
entitled *A Record of Guizhou Province* enumerated eighty-two, as does
the album reproduced below.[46] As the system of naming became
increasingly elaborate, the geographical scope of inquiry also expanded.
Later works contain references to remote areas of the province not mentioned earlier. Furthermore, the amount of ethnographic detail was con-
tinually augmented up until about 1750, presumably on the basis of direct
observation.[47] Publications like these, portions of which described the
customs (*fengsu*) of non-Chinese inhabitants of the province, formed
the textual basis for the Miao albums.

   The text of the album reproduced here uses a number of approaches
to define and describe the peoples it depicts. In unpacking its meaning, it may be helpful to think of the textual content as comprising four
different types of maps or diagrams, all superimposed on one other.
I will describe each approach separately, in much the same way that
one can individually view anatomical transparencies showing different body parts and bodily systems before again layering them on top
of one another for added "real life" complexity.

The first "map" or diagram seeks to order the multiplicity of culturally non-Chinese peoples resident in Guizhou through an elaborate taxonomy. Each page of text begins with a numbered heading that gives the name of the group to be described. In this way, the unwieldy ethnic and cultural diversity of the province is broken down into smaller parts that are thus made knowable. The organization of the album further reflects this taxonomy, giving it substance.

The system of naming has its own internal logic. The names of the peoples depicted generally consist of two parts. One identifies the larger ethnic group, that is, Miao, Gelao, Luoluo, Zhongjia, and so on. Many of these general categories are still in use today, although some of them have been renamed; Zhongjia and Luoluo (that appear in the albums) have been superseded by Buyi and Yi respectively.[48] The other part of the name serves as a modifier, providing more intricate classifications within ethnicities. These distinctions, which have since been rejected by anthropologists and ethnologists who find them both superficial and unhelpful, were often based on some aspect of appearance, or other distinct practices or characteristics. Red (fig. 14), White (fig. 15), Blue (fig. 16), Black (fig. 17) and Flowery Miao (fig. 13) were, for example, named for the color of their garb. Pointed-Head Miao (fig. 78); Pot-Ring Gelao (fig. 28 and pl. 3); and Dog-Eared (fig. 10), Stirrup (fig. 11), and Large-Headed Longjia (fig. 12) for their hairstyles or head coverings (see also pls. 9 and 10). Pig-Filth Gelao (fig. 24) were said to go for a year without bathing. Water Gelao (fig. 27) were known for their aquatic skill, and Wild or Raw Miao (fig. 74) for their untamed nature. Not all of the names are so transparent, nor is it possible to determine all of their derivations or how each relates to the fifty-five minority nationalities currently recognized in China today. Some names may have been transliterations from non-Chinese languages.

The second way the information in the texts served as a kind of map was to plot the location of the various groups onto the political geography of the province. The location in which a given group resided is almost always identified at the outset of the description. Location was indicated by administrative divisions such as prefecture, district, subdistrict, or military encampment. The group's provenance, if known, was also recorded. Provincial administrators could thus conceptually map peoples in a way that corresponded to what they already knew. Such geographical mapping also allowed officials to correlate which geographically remote frontier areas were culturally foreign or inhospitable, and which areas were more amenable to imperial rule.

Most, if not all, of the album texts describe the clothing worn by both men and women in some detail, providing a third means by which peoples could be identified. The ability to visually recognize and categorize the different groups was important because people did, of course, travel and could not be relied on to verbally self-identify, particularly according to the categories created by Chinese officialdom. Visual identification of ethnicity based on costume allowed the viewer to slot a person into a mental category that corresponded with the album's taxonomy. The ability to categorically identify a person through their appearance was another way to order one's cultural environment.[49]

Finally, the texts served as a kind of indicator of where the groups fell on a cultural continuum from "like us" (*yu hanren tong*) to savage or in some way "Other." This kind of distancing did not involve a simple dualistic conception of barbarian versus civilized, but rather a more complex system in which a group's distance from a cultural center was measured by examining the specifics of its cultural practices.[50]

Significantly, the albums show how this formation of Han identity began well *before* the recognized penetration of Western-based forms of nationalism into China.[51] Areas of ethnographic inquiry tended to correspond to those realms of life where prescribed ritual practices (*li*) determined what was civilized according to Chinese Confucian culture—including courtship practices and marriage customs, death ritual, religious practices, and the observance of festivals.[52] While less prominent as a category of inquiry, diet was also sometimes described. Other general topics for consideration included whether members of the group could speak or understand Chinese, how a group earned its livelihood, and any other particularly remarkable habits or beliefs. Some texts go so far as to attribute a certain "nature" to the members of a given group such as "honest and careful," "crafty and fierce," "nimble and cruel," or "unyielding and foolish." Not every entry covers all of these topics.

As with any ethnographic text, we learn not only about the peoples described, but also about the authors' interests and preoccupations. Thus, in reading the cultural maps provided by the albums we must always be conscious of a kind of doubleness ingrained in the texts. Just as historians need to carefully interpret the documents they use to distinguish the "facts" they contain from the attitudes of the authors who recorded them, we need to read the ethnographic information in the albums with care. While we should not dismiss all of the content out of hand as biased or voyeuristic, we do need to keep in mind that the content was necessarily mediated by the lenses through which the authors viewed and understood their subjects.[53] While the term "information" can be used to describe the albums' contents, it should not be understood as an uncritical acceptance of the veracity of all the recorded details. Rather, the word primarily reflects the state of knowledge in a given place at a given time. The "information" in the albums was undoubtedly flawed, just as all our knowledge is flawed to some degree through the limitations posed by our own inevitable subjectivity. This is why scholarship is constantly revised. The following pages take a close look at the customs described in the albums. Although we may think that excessive interest is shown in certain areas such as sexuality or death ritual, keeping in mind both what we can learn about the peoples described, and about those describing them, helps us more fully understand these preoccupations.

Courtship rituals and marriage customs, as well as norms that governed the relationship between the bride and groom and their extended families, attracted the most attention. In a culture where arranged marriages and patrilineal descent were the norm, variant practices understandably held a fascination for those to whom they were forbidden. Among Guizhou's ethnic minorities, courtship practices often centered around an annual festival, usually held in the spring, at which young men and women had the opportunity to interact and subsequently to select partners. The Kayou Zhongjia (fig. 6), as discussed above, held a spring moon dance at which young women would toss a colorful ball to their partner of choice. The Hua Miao (fig. 13) and Bai Miao (fig. 15) also held moon dances in the spring, at which the women shook bells and the men played a reed wind instrument called a *lüsheng*. Each spring, the Gou'er Longjia youth (fig. 10) would dance around a "ghost" pole, resembling a May pole, as part of their courtship activities. The Qingjiang Hei Miao (fig. 56) are described as picnicking together in the woods where they would also sing and dance. Couples signified their commitment by sharing an ox horn cup. The New Year's festival was a time for the Liuzhong Miao (fig. 26) to pair off; the woman being carried off on the back of her lover.

Parents tended to support the youth in what are sometimes described as "illicit" activities. Among the Bazhai Miao (fig. 55), each village would erect a building where the youth would come together to choose their mates. The Yao Miao (fig. 20) also had courting houses for their young where men could woo young women by playing music on reed pipes. Young Qing Zhongjia couples (fig. 8) would sneak off to go drinking together before marriage. Although parents did not forbid the practice, girls had to hide it from their brothers. Betrothal arrangements were arrived at only after couples had engaged in sexual intercourse. Practices among the Gaopo Miao (fig. 60) are described as being even more informal; marriage was simply determined by who decided to sleep together. In most cases, betrothal arrangements concerning dowry or bride price were to be worked out after couples had chosen each other—or even given birth to a first child as in the case of the Lingjia Miao (fig. 46) and Xiqi Miao (fig. 72). Only the Yangbao Miao (fig. 37) and Gulin Miao (fig. 42) are described as using a matchmaker in the more conventional sense.

According to the albums, the degree of freedom one had for choosing one's own mate varied extensively among the groups. Women from some groups were free even to have relations with Han men. Turen women (fig. 33), for example, are described as intermarrying with both soldiers and commoners. Bai Zhongjia women (fig. 67) could also court outsiders. However, the text indicates that these relationships were often eventually broken off. Having had such a liaison did not, apparently, prevent the woman from making a good marriage from within her own ethnic group at a later date. This would have been unheard of in China's dominant culture where chastity was all important; Qing biographies of virtuous women even included examples of young women who refused to marry at all after the death of their betrothed. Not all ethnic groups enjoyed so much marital freedom. Yetou Miao women (fig. 53) were expected to marry a son of a maternal uncle, or to pay off his family.

While generally speaking the courtship and marriage practices described in the album are much freer than those dictated by Chinese Confucian culture, various groups described had their own sometimes restrictive practices. The Daya Gelao (fig. 22) chiseled off the bride's front teeth so that she would not bring harm to her husband's family. Among the Caijia Miao (fig. 5), fathers and daughters-in-law were forbidden to speak to one another. Even more drastically, the text relates that, "When the husband dies the wife is buried alive with him unless her family rescues her." Among the Zijiang Miao (fig. 41), by contrast, widows were required to remarry before the bodies of their deceased husbands were buried. Inclusion of examples of such extreme cases of violence against women allowed the Chinese to construct themselves as a civilized center. A number of unspoken messages come through: While Han women did not enjoy certain freedoms, they were also protected from certain forms of violence. Similarly, if Han men were less driven by raw sexuality, they were also less prone to brutality. Of course, both of these messages reflected views from a constructed cultural center, and could be challenged from a number of angles.

Second to courtship and marriage, death rituals claim the most consistent attention in the album texts. This is no coincidence for, as James Watson has put it, "the proper performance of the rites . . . was of paramount importance in determining who was and who was not deemed to be fully 'Chinese.'"[54] In the albums, topics relating to death ritual include what was done with the corpse, what kind of mourning or other rituals were held, beliefs surrounding the deceased, and—in at least one instance—remarriage of widows. The treatment is anecdotal rather than systematic. We learn, for example, that the Langci Miao (fig. 79) twisted the heads of their dead around immediately after death so that the deceased could keep an eye on their descendants from the afterlife. This same text, however, gives no indications as to whether the corpse was then buried and, if so, whether or not a coffin of some sort was used. Even assuming the reliability of the texts, which is open to question, this kind of sketchy evidence limits the albums' usefulness as source material. One cannot determine, for example, the percentage of groups in Guizhou that buried their dead.

Although the albums do not always answer the questions we might want to ask, they do nonetheless record a fair amount of ethnographic detail. A good example is the coverage of a wide variety of practices for disposing of a corpse. The Bai Luoluo (fig. 3) would wrap the dead body in animal hides and burn it. The Cengzhu Longjia (fig. 9) burned the body, buried the bones, and followed up by performing annual sacrifices to the dead on the seventh day of the seventh month. The Hua Miao (fig. 13) buried their dead without using coffins, having first determined an auspicious site through a ritual that involved throwing a chicken. The Ge Zhuang (fig. 31) also buried their dead without coffins, instead laying the body out on a plank, while the Pingfa Miao (fig. 61) used a wooden trough. The Gelao (fig. 25) did use coffins, but did not bury them; they rather placed them in a cave or a forested area near a river. The Yaque Miao (fig. 69) would select a mountain top location as an auspicious spot for burial. The Liu Ezi (fig. 49) used coffins in burial, but then dug up the bones annually for seven years in order to wash them clean. If illness struck the family it was attributed to the bones not having been scrubbed clean enough. In such cases, the bones would then be dug up for additional cleansing even after the seven year period was over. The Louju Hei Miao (fig. 57) used coffins, but would delay burial for up to twenty years, until they could bury a great number of bodies together at the same time. In conjunction with the burial they would collectively build an ancestral hall. The Yao Miao (fig. 20), by contrast, neither used coffins nor practiced burial. They would tie the corpse up in a tree and allow the elements to transform it gradually.

The albums' authors were attentive to social and religious rituals surrounding death as well as to burial practices. A number of groups would hold a big gathering following a death. Beyond the general ethnographic interest this information held for cultural mapping, administrators in the area might find it useful to know which minority groups would congregate when a death occurred. In the context of recent and potential rebellion, the assembly of large groups could make officials nervous. As one might expect, practices at such funeral gatherings varied. The Bulong Zhongjia (fig. 7) are said to have served meat to their guests with the host generally eating fish or shrimp instead. The Dong Miao (fig. 18) would slaughter a water buffalo, sacrificially prepare the meat, and call out to the deceased. Afterward all would partake, drink, and sing. Manren (fig. 34) practices are similarly described. The Hong Miao (fig. 14) made a likeness of the deceased by stuffing clothing and then would "sing, drum, and dance." The Kemeng Guyang Miao (fig. 43) would also throw a party for the deceased, delaying their mourning until the following spring when the cry of the cuckoo would remind the family that although the birds return annually, the dead cannot.

Not all groups held feasts or parties in conjunction with funerals. The Bafan Miao (fig. 40) preferred to bury their dead quietly at night. Some groups reflected mourning through their dress. The Madeng Longjia (fig. 11) wore dark clothes instead of white during mourning—a reversal from Han practices. The Mulao (fig. 30) also demonstrated their grief through a change in their outward appearance; what they wore is not described, the reader is simply told that it was not coarse white hemp, as was customary among the Han.

The albums also prominently describe seasonal festivals and religious practices. The dominant Chinese culture observed several festivals, which were tied to the lunar cycle. The most important may have been the celebration of the New Year, followed (in calendrical order) by the Lantern Festival, Qing Ming (or Grave-Sweeping Day), Dragon Boat Festival, and the Mid-Autumn Moon Festival. The Miao albums detail which of the festivals were also observed by the peoples described (for some held at different times), and which were not.

A number of Guizhou's minority groups held observances foreign to their Chinese neighbors. The Liuzhong Miao (fig. 26), Yaoren (fig. 36), and Lingjia Miao (fig. 46) all worshiped Pan Hu as part of their New Year's celebrations. Pan Hu is a legendary figure, in the form of a dog, whose union with a Chinese princess is supposed to have given birth to the Yao. The Bai Miao (fig. 15) and Dong Miao (fig. 18) both performed annual sacrifices to their ancestors. The Manren (fig. 34) were said to "perform sacrifices to ghosts" on the first day of the tenth month. Whether these were the ghosts of their ancestors is not made clear. Some groups had beliefs that were unique to them. The Hong Miao (fig. 14) would sleep separately on the first day of the fifth month, and stay inside in order to "avoid ghosts and tigers." The Zijiang Miao (fig. 41) had a week-long prohibition on going out during the eleventh month. The Xi Miao (fig. 19) would hold a three-day festival after the autumn harvest when they would offer sacrifices to a "white tiger," make music, and dance. They also celebrated the Spring Festival with chicken and wine. The festivities celebrated by the Bai Zhongjia (fig. 67) in spring seem to have centered around courtship activities; no mention of sacrifices or offerings is made at all. For some groups such as the Yao Miao (fig. 20), Boren (fig. 32), Bafan Miao (fig. 40), and Jiantou Miao (fig. 78), the date of their big festival is given, but no additional detail. The Liminzi (fig. 64) are said to have New Year's rites and festivals "similar to those of the Han."

In some instances, religious beliefs and practices are mentioned in contexts where specific annual festivals are not recounted. The Louju Hei Miao (fig. 57) are described as being respectful of ghosts, not daring to infringe on the land set aside for the "ghost hall." The Luoluo (fig. 1) also believed in ghosts, although no additional detail is given. The Boren (fig. 32) and Luohan Miao (fig. 80) are depicted as adherents of Maitreya Buddha. Most albums, like the one reproduced here, show them worshiping before a Buddhist altar. The Guoquan Gelao (fig. 28) would fashion a tiger head from flour paste, decorate it with colorful thread, and engage a shaman to pray when a person fell ill (see also pl. 3). When sacrificing to ghosts, the Mulao (fig. 30) would make a dragon from straw, and insert five flags, each of a different color, into its back. The Bai Longjia (fig. 66) offered a conundrum. Their weddings and funerals followed Han rites, but they wore white on a daily basis. Han Chinese associate the color white with mourning. The reader is also informed about contradictory aspects of the Yangbao Miao (fig. 37). Although "their sacrifices are also like Han rituals," they are described as "crafty and fierce" by nature. Theoretically, practicing such Confucian rites should have produced a corresponding civilizing effect on their behaviors.

Diet was another cultural marker of civilization.[55] Generally diet is remarked on only when it is somehow exceptional; most often as an indication of the degree of a group's savagery. The Sheng Miao (fig. 74) would "generally . . . eat any living thing." Their name, "Raw" or "Wild" Miao, is said to derive from their belief that "half-cooked fish and meat are the most delicious foods." The Zhushi Gelao (fig. 24) were said to gnaw noisily on the animals they caught, "just like a wolf would." The Hei Miao (fig. 17) were described as being so debased that they had to use bracken ash instead of salt, and considered putrefied meat a delicacy. The Bai Luoluo (fig. 3) would "collect and cook any animal that wriggles or moves, including rodents, birds, and insect larvae," and eat it, without utensils, from a common pot. The Hong Miao (fig. 14) were noted for eating their meat extremely rare. "Using fire to remove the hair, they cook the meat only slightly and eat it while it is still bloody." More neutral images of diet also appear in the Miao albums, although less often. Peculiarities were specifically noted: the Dongren (fig. 35) avoided salt in their diet, the Qian Miao (fig. 45) ate some hemp seed, the Ranjia Man (fig. 51) considered shrimp and fish a delicacy, while the Shuijia Miao (fig. 48) were noted for their diet of glutinous rice and water.

Language facility, like rites and diet, was another way to gauge the degree of cultural distance that non-Han ethnic groups occupied from the center. Although the written Chinese word (*wen*) was literally synonymous with culture, in this context the spoken language most obviously divided members of minority ethnic groups from neighboring speakers of Chinese—of whatever dialect. The Songjia Miao (fig. 4) were said to be conversant in Chinese, the Dongjia Miao (fig. 47) could speak but not read it, and the Zhushi Gelao (fig. 24) and Dong Miao (fig. 44) understood it. Boren (fig. 32) were known for being conversant in all of the Miao languages. The language of the Yaque Miao (fig. 69) was said to "resemble the sounds of small birds."

How different peoples passed their time and earned a living was also of interest. Most groups are described as either tillers and weavers, or hunters, or some combination of both. The Gulin Miao (fig. 42) and Hongzhou Miao (fig. 71) were famous for the fine cloth woven by the women. The Kemeng Guyang Miao (fig. 43) and Dongjia Miao (fig. 47) were known for raising cotton, the Duanqun Miao (fig. 77) for harvesting gromwell, a plant producing purple dye, while the Hulu (fig. 70), Hei Jiao (fig. 75), and Hei Shan Miao (fig. 58) were singled out as relying on robbery for their livelihoods. Although Qingjiang Zhongjia males (fig. 63) would kidnap and hold unwary travelers for ransom, the women were described as "diligent at both weaving and working in the fields." Participation in trade or skilled labor distinguished a number of groups. The Qingjiang Hei Miao (fig. 56) and Hei Zhongjia (fig. 59) both raised trees, and had business dealings with the Han. The latter group would also act as money lenders, and had a reputation for ruthlessness if cheated. They would take revenge by digging up "the bones of the guarantor's ancestors" thus forcing repayment. Yaoren (fig. 36) collected medicinal herbs and practiced healing arts. The Bai Longjia (fig. 66) collected medicinal herbs in the mountains, and cut down lacquer trees to sell in the market. The Liminzi (fig. 64) engaged in trade, some Bai Luoluo (fig. 3) dealt in tea, and the Pipao Gelao (fig. 29) cast ploughshares for a living.

Not all of the information contained in the albums falls neatly into the broad categories described above. Other topics that come up include governance, conflict resolution, class relationships, the physical setting in which different groups prefer to live, common surnames (if used), the practice of divination, and a myriad other observations that the reader will discover in perusing the translation.

In addition to these textual descriptions, the album reproduced here also contains a poem on each page. Poetry appears only in a small percentage of the extant Miao albums. When it does, it occupies an intermediary space between the prose text and the illustrations. Not only are the poems located literally between the prose text and the pictures, but by using words to create images, they create further room for interpretation in the mind of the beholder. The poetry thus provides an additional avenue for enriching, and perhaps exoticizing, the picture of each group portrayed.

The poems express a wide range of emotion and imagery. Some, like those reflecting on the Gaopo Miao (fig. 60) and Jiantou Miao (fig. 78) paint an idyllic, if bucolic, setting. These poems evoke images of rural tranquility, plenty, and matrimonial harmony. Others are belittling, or derogatory, as in the cases of the Yaque Miao (fig. 69) and Sheng Miao (fig. 74). "Completely unintelligible," the speech of the Yaque Miao is "Amusing, like cawing crows and chirping sparrows." In a standard four-character expression used to evoke savagery, the reader is told that for the Sheng Miao, "Munching fur and quaffing blood are customary," their primitive eating habits apparently unaffected by civilization. Poems are also used to pose a conundrum or to explain something that might otherwise not be apparent: Why is it that the Bai Longjia (fig. 66) "customarily wear white, / Yet in weddings and funerals imitate the Han?" It would appear that the Hei Zhongjia (fig. 59) have a fierce reputation, but then, "only because many Han fail to meet their debts / Are the bones of the guarantor's ancestors harmed." In each instance, the imagery is rich, complementing the accompanying illustration, even as it creates a space for the mind to embroider its own variations on the themes provided.

EARLY MODERN ETHNOGRAPHY

Since the appearance of Edward Said's *Orientalism* in 1979, Euro-American representations of "Others" have attracted increasing amounts of critical attention.[56] However, non-Western representations of their "Others" are only beginning to be examined, especially for the early modern period.[57] The emergence of early modern ethnographic practices *across* cultures has been difficult to see for a number of reasons. Post-colonial theory has linked technologies of representation, including both cartography and early ethnographic practice, to the rise of merchant capitalism and colonialism among emergent European nation states. In this context, studies of the age of exploration have focused primarily on describing the rise of Western hegemony and local forms of resistance to it. Not surprisingly, critiques of Western hegemony have been largely shaped by, or in reaction to, the grand narrative of the "rise of the West."[58] However, for this reason, the very possibility of "non-Western" colonialism is only beginning to be considered.[59] At base is a binary division in our thinking that has too long allowed "Western" and, by implication, "non-Western" or "Other" to be accepted as legitimate descriptive categories that function as a shorthand for a wide set of cultural practices and assumptions, rather than terms primarily signifying place.[60] The situation is compounded by a (now-fading) disciplinary bias toward national histories in the academy, and the practical difficulty of conducting research in different parts of the world in a variety of languages—both of which make it difficult to carry out broad comparative historical studies involving regions construed as part of the "non-West."

Although little studied to date, expanding non-Western empires also engaged in ethnographic representation. The following examples of ethnographic representation from Tokugawa Japan (1603–1867) and the Ottoman empire (c. 1300–1922) place the Miao albums in comparative historical perspective. During the early modern period, the Tokugawa state was consolidating its rule over Japan, establishing firm borders, and defining itself in relation to other parts of the world. The Ottoman empire, like China, extended its power over a vast multi-ethnic domain, and engaged in extensive trade and cultural relationships beyond its borders. These relatively far-flung examples demonstrate that during the early modern period, a variety of states in different parts of the world were consolidating their knowledge of and control over peripheral peoples and territories.[61] Examining comparative models of representation of "Others" brings a more balanced world-historical perspective to a consideration of the early modern period.

Ainu-e: Japanese Illustrations of the Ainu People

The Tokugawa period in Japan saw the rise of a genre of illustrated albums depicting culturally distinct peoples living on the periphery of the state. Because the Japanese albums depict the northern Ainu peoples from the island of Hokkaido, they are known as *Illustrations of the Ainu* (Ainu-e). Like the Chinese Miao albums, *Ainu-e* are the cultural prod-

ucts of a transitional period in which the state was working to consol-
idate its rule over different peoples and territories that had earlier
enjoyed a greater degree of autonomy.[62]

The large island of Ezo—later renamed Hokkaido—was not initially
ruled directly by the Tokugawa shogunate, but by the Matsumae, one
of many *daimyo* families, or vassals. Members of this family, whose
wealth and legitimacy depended on trade and other relations with the
Ainu, first collected information about them.[63] Following the sup-
pression of an Ainu rebellion in 1669, the Matsumae family imposed
certain rituals on the Ainu with whom they demanded exclusive trad-
ing privileges. For the Matsumae, these ritual practices, known as
uimam, marked a tributary relationship in which the Ainu recognized
the political authority of the Matsumae and signified their own submission.[64] The Ainu, however, viewed the "audience" simply as an
opportunity for trade.[65] Gradually, the Tokugawa shogunate asserted
its direct control over Hokkaido, partly in response to Russia's perceived
territorial aspirations. In the emergent system of nation states, the existence of multiple sovereignties and power sharing with vassals or other
intermediaries could not be tolerated. From this time forward, the
shogunate developed a keen interest in the Ainu, who were seen as
potential allies against Russian encroachment.[66]

While some artistic depictions of Ainu had been made before the
eighteenth century, the term *Ainu-e* refers specifically to those illustrations of Ainu that appeared after the 1720 publication of *Ezo-shi*, a
gazetteer of Ezo by Arai Hakuseki (1656–1720).[67] This gazetteer was
followed by an appendix containing illustrations of Ainu made from
live models.[68] Much as the imperially commissioned illustrations in
the Kangxi-era Guizhou gazetteers (1673, 1692) were the starting point
for the Miao albums, the illustrated appendix to the *Ezo-shi* may have
formed the initial basis for the illustrations of the *Ainu-e*.[69] The author
may even have been acquainted with the common practice of including a section on "customs" in local gazetteers. Educated Japanese would
have been familiar with Chinese literary and historical genres. In fact,
the *Ezo-shi* contains allusions to the Chinese *Classic of Mountains and
Seas*, and to the Tang and Song histories.[70] However, there is no reason to believe that Arai would have been exposed to the Miao albums
themselves.

During the eighteenth and nineteenth centuries, *Ainu-e* were made in significant numbers. The albums went by a wide variety of titles,[71] and were produced by a number of different artists.[72] Some took the form of scrolls, and others that of books. As one would expect, they differ in organization and content from the Chinese Miao albums in a number of ways. Because the *Ainu-e* focus on only one ethnic group, illustrations are devoted to different aspects of Ainu culture and to a variety of cultural activities, rather than to different ethnic subgroups as in the Miao albums. One scroll, for example, begins with a recounting of the Ainu foundation myth. The Ainu are described here as the progeny of a female spirit from overseas and a dog who cared for her after she arrived by boat. The origin myth is followed by annotated illustrations of a man and a woman, objects for bodily adornment (including tattoos), distinctive customs, objects representing Ainu material culture, their dwelling places, and religious practices.[73] *Portraits of Ezo Chieftains*, which are also considered *Ainu-e*, are reminiscent of the *Qing Imperial Illustrations of Tributary Peoples*; each page contains an illustration of one figure in native costume, clearly labeled.[74] Plate 12 reproduces an illustration from an *Ainu-e*.

Like the Miao albums, the *Ainu-e* were frequently recopied, sometimes by artists who clearly did not understand what they were drawing, sometimes by artists who added their own interpretive gestures. Thus, like the Chinese Miao albums, some may be more reliable as ethnographic source material than others.[75] In both cases, it was no coincidence that those who compiled the ethnographic information were peoples of a different culture and ethnicity who were also in a position of authority over the peoples and lands portrayed. Both the *Ainu-e* and the Miao albums demonstrate that ethnographic depiction was not the sole province of European expansion.

Ethnographic Representation in Ottoman Art

If ethnographic depiction was not confined to the "West" but was also a feature of early modern state building in East Asia, was it present in other contexts as well? To address this question, let us turn to the Ottoman empire. To date, Ottoman ethnography has not been an area of scholarly inquiry for a number of reasons. In most circles, ethnography is still thought of as having developed in the "West," whether as part or product of Western colonial pursuits. Furthermore, it is sometimes popularly presumed that techniques of realistic representation

Plate 12. Illustration from an Ainu album. University of Pennsylvania Museum, neg. T4–3200.

did not take hold because of Islamic resistance to the making of graven images. Only Allah could create; artists were to represent ideal images, but not to represent individuals, whether humans or animals.[76] Yet visual and textual representations of actual locations and peoples were central to imperially sponsored Ottoman art for centuries.

From before the time of Süleyman the Magnificent (r. 1520–1566), an imperial workshop known as the *nakkaşhane* recorded significant events in the history of the empire. The workshop, administratively attached to the military, produced illuminated manuscripts of the life of the sultan; genealogies of the sultans; and books recording and visually depicting festivals and special ceremonial occasions such as visits from foreign ambassadors and the circumcision of royal sons. Campaign histories depicting battle scenes were painted on-site. Furthermore, specific locations reached by military campaigns were also recorded in sketches.[77] Although texts were an important part of these works, reproductions generally only depict the artwork. The text of the *Süleymānnāme*, a record of the reign of Süleyman I from 1520 to 1558, is written in verse.[78] From these examples, we can determine that visual records of the Ottoman empire were important during the early modern period, whether or not they specifically distinguished and identified particular groups of peoples by ethnic origin.

In the early decades of the eighteenth century, Abdulcelil Çelebi, more commonly known as Levni, painted illustrations for a number of books and albums remarkable for their ethnographic qualities. His illustrations in the *Book of Circumcision* (Surname-i Vehbi) show tremendous detail in terms of palace architecture, hierarchy of officials, and variety of occupation and dress among commoners. Depiction of European diplomats who attended the ceremony is also extremely detailed. Even more directly ethnographic are illustrations for his *Murakka* or "album," that include not only various figures from the palace court, but also foreigners including Europeans. An annotation accompanying an illustration labeled "Austrian" remarks on the beauty of the young man. His female counterpart is also pictured in the album. A poem accompanying the images informs the reader that wine is responsible for the color of their complexions. Beyond the broad category of "Austrians," the individuals are not identified.[79]

Levni's subject matter, the relatively "realistic" style of his work, and the fact that he painted in the early eighteenth century during a period when the court was taking a renewed interest in the outside world, might lead one to believe that he was influenced by European models. However, other, probably older, indigenous examples of this kind of pictorial representation—that could be described as "ethnographic"— exist as well. The collection of Arabic manuscripts in the Bibliothèque nationale in Paris houses four albums containing, among other illustrations, paintings of a single figure, or sometimes two, in distinctive dress, sometimes carrying an object associated with his or her station in life. Famous princes and princesses are portrayed, but also officers, mullahs, Indian ascetics, dervishes, the executioner of the sultan, a cupbearer, a water carrier, musicians, and even a veiled woman holding the hand of a young child. Many of the paintings, which are in the Safavid style, are labeled in Persian, and some include poetic inscriptions. Each is bordered with fine handiwork displaying the skills and techniques of the trained manuscript illuminator. Their general style of composition, although not their specific content, is reminiscent of the *Qing Imperial Illustrations of Tributary Peoples*. Although the specific origins of these album leaves are uncertain, Persian artists were patronized at the Ottoman court (see pls. 13 and 14).[80]

Some of the illustrations in these albums show a close connection to two somewhat later works housed in the Print Room (Département des Estampes) of the Bibliothèque nationale. The first, dated 1688, is comprised of a total of sixty illustrations. According to the catalog, the paintings were made in Turkey by a native artist and then pasted into an album under a French title. Figures from the Ottoman court, residents of Constantinople, and scenes from daily life are all depicted with close attention to detail.[81] One illustration depicts a woman making a pilgrimage to Mecca, another, a troupe of acrobats. Foreigners are also shown, including dervishes from India, Persia, and Europe. Alternate pages contain explanatory texts in French. The name or title of the person described is printed in red, and a description of the role of that person in black ink. Each illustration is set off by a rectangular border, but one that is plainer than those described above. Comparing the album page reproduced in plate 15 with plate 13 gives one a sense of the similarities between the Arabic and European albums, and also of the derivative nature of the latter. Its quality is inferior to the album leaves in the collection of Arabic manuscripts.

The other album, dating from 1720, is actually bilingual. While there

Plate 13. A Prince with Falcon. Bibliothèque nationale de France, Ms. Arabe 6076.

Plate 14. Executioner of the Sultan. Bibliothèque nationale de France, Ms. Arabe 6077.

Plate 15. "Dogandgi," the Page who Carried the Sultan's Falcon. Bibliothèque nationale de France, Département des Estampes, Od 7.

is less text, each illustration is labeled in both Arabic script and French (see pl. 16).[82] The illustrations are similar, but not identical, to the 1688 manuscript and there is evidence that its contents, too, are probably derivative of older indigenous albums. To cite one example, we see repeated here the depiction of a veiled woman holding a child's hand. The French inscription describes the plainly dressed woman as a slave accompanying her mistress. The Print Room also contains a number of earlier European manuscripts painted in a style similar to those described here.[83]

Most fascinating with regard to this foray into Ottoman ethnographic representation is the interplay between Ottoman and French art and sources. We see evidence of borrowing between the Ottoman and French works, but also of joint production in those that were commissioned by Europeans, drawn by Turkish artists, and then circulated in Europe, sometimes in bilingual editions. Furthermore, it would seem that in their thirst for information about the Ottoman empire, Europeans drew from existing Ottoman art forms as source material for their own ethnographic inquiry. Thus, portraits of individuals would be copied and later labeled in such a way that their specific identities were lost, even as categorical labels, such as "falconer," were created.[84]

There is also a lesson here about how the conclusions we draw are affected by what we see, which is, in turn, influenced by how manuscripts are housed and catalogued. After looking at only the Print Room manuscripts, one might simply conclude that the French had a long history of interest in learning about Turkish people and the workings of the Turkish court, and that this may only have been picked up on by the Ottomans in the late seventeenth or early eighteenth century—judging by when we see bilingual and joint-made manuscripts, as well as Levni's paintings of foreigners. However, when viewing the album leaves in the Arabic collection, it becomes evident that indigenous works made with superior artistry also existed contemporaneously, and may even have predated what were probably European copies.[85]

From what little we know of this imperially sponsored art, it is still premature to claim the definitive existence of as developed an ethnography in the Ottoman empire as we see in Qing China. However, Ottoman artists were certainly taking an interest in different kinds of peoples, their dress, provenance, occupation, and station in life. The work sponsored by the *nakkaşhane*, Levni's *Murakka*, and the albums described

Plate 16. Badanadgi, or an Armenian Who Whitewashed Walls. Bibliothèque nationale de France, Département des Estampes, Od 6.

above do show that at least a nascent ethnography did exist and suggest that the time is ripe for further inquiry into this area.

The hand-painted illustrated ethnographies of peoples on China's southwestern frontier reproduced in the body of this book, the Japanese *Ainu-e*, and the examples of Ottoman ethnographic representation are, of course, different from each other in important ways, but are also broadly comparable. They helped members of their intended audience to conceptualize, categorize, and learn about "Other" peoples in distant lands, or remote parts of their own country. These representations included both representatives of established states as well as frontier peoples who were targeted for closer control. Although Euro-American representation of "Others" has, to date, been given more scholarly attention, this analysis shows that expanding states and empires in other parts of the early modern world also collected ethnographic information about peripheral peoples as they tightened control over them. Illustrated ethnographic albums are part and parcel of an ethnography of expansion that emerged worldwide during the early modern period. They sometimes romanticized the primitive or exotic, and at other times portrayed a more menacing picture. The Miao album reproduced in this book can help modern readers understand that ethnographic depiction was not solely the province of the early modern "West," and that cultural difference and its management has long been a preoccupation of the state worldwide.

NOTES

1. See, for example, Alloula, *The Colonial Harem*; Asad, *Anthropology and the Colonial Encounter*; Bucher, *Icon and Conquest*; Clifford, *The Predicament of Culture*; Gilman, *Difference and Pathology*; Hodgen, *Early Anthropology*; Pratt, *Imperial Eyes*; and Said, *Orientalism*.

2. These groups are only "minorities" when considered in relation to the Qing polity as a whole. In the regions in which they lived they most often constituted majorities.

3. By China proper, I refer to those areas governed under the Ming dynasty.

4. These are reproduced in Chuang, *Xie Sui "zhigong tu"*; see also his "Xie Sui zhigong tu yanjiu." For representations of Europeans, see Hostetler, "Qing Views of Europeans." Numerous versions of the *Qing Imperial Illustrations of Tributary Peoples* are extant.

5. That is to say that their primary ethnic and cultural identity was not with the dominant Chinese culture.

6. *Daqing lichao shilu*, 390:8–9. See also Hostetler, *Qing Colonial Enterprise*, 46.

7. For a book-length study on the Miao album genre and the context in which it arose, see Hostetler, *Qing Colonial Enterprise*.

8. Hostetler, "Qing Connections," 623–62.

9. This is not to say that *all* genres of earlier writing about other peoples were necessarily without any basis in direct observation. Work is currently being undertaken for earlier periods. See, e.g., Brose, "Realism and Idealism."

10. *Huang Qing zhigong tu*, Introduction (*ti yao*), 2. See also Jaeger, "Über Chinesische Miaotse-Albums," 82–83.

11. *Secret Palace Memorials*. Memorial dated the seventeenth day of the eleventh month of the sixteenth year of the Qianlong emperor's reign (1751). See also Hostetler, *Qing Colonial Enterprise*, 45.

12. *Secret Palace Memorials*.

13. Preface to *Bai Miao tu yong*. This album is dated 1890, which is quite late in the development of the genre. See Hostetler, *Qing Colonial Enterprise*, 165, for a translation of a portion of this preface. Very few albums contain prefatory material of any kind.

14. We do not have the drafts from which Xie Sui produced *Huang Qing zhigong tu*.

15. The dating of the album was determined by an analysis of place names appearing in the text. Yongfeng Department (*zhou*) was renamed Zhenfeng in 1797. Zhenfeng appears in this album's descriptive passages for both the Nong Miao and the Bai Ezi.

16. For a color reproduction and translation of a forty-page album in the British Library's collection, along with additional album pages selected from the same collection, see Tapp and Cohn, *Tribal Peoples of Southwest China*.

17. The album reproduced here is missing two pages of text, those describing the Chezhai Miao (fig. 73), and the Liudong Yiren (fig. 82) respectively. The texts for these entries have been translated from other albums.

18. Although it could be argued that North American depictions of Native Americans bear important similarities in goals and content to the ethnographies discussed here, they are not included. The goal here is to elucidate non-Western examples of the ethnography of expansion.

19. It is premature to say whether the range of examples of ethnographic representation discussed here arose independently or influenced each other. This is also, perhaps, not the most relevant or useful line of inquiry. Like concepts of "West" and "non-West," the dualism invoked by such a question exists more clearly in the mind than in actual practice. By concerning ourselves too much with cultural or national origins, we undercut the possibility of a complex interplay of ideas and practices that may lead, even independently, to similar pursuits (although possibly for different reasons). An exclusive search for models (as *are* sometimes found, as we shall see below) does not grant the possibility of fruitful cross-fertilization, tending instead to relegate the "copier" to imitator status, thereby precluding the possibility of independent creative thought and invention.

20. For more on the *tusi* system, see Herman, "Empire in the Southwest"; and Herman, "National Hegemony and Regional Hegemony."

21. Many of these specific restrictions were lifted by his successor, who also

allowed local disputes to be resolved through traditional channels. For more on *gaitu guiliu* and specific policies in Guizhou under the Yongzheng emperor, see Smith, "Ch'ing Policy." On restrictions under the Yongzheng emperor, see Lombard-Salmon, *Un exemple d'acculturation chinoise*, 222, 232.

22. See Teng, *Taiwan's Imagined Geography*; and Song Guangyu, *Huanan bian-jiang*.

23. See Hostetler, *Qing Colonial Enterprise*; and Tapp and Cohn, *Tribal Peoples of Southwest China*. Other works on Guizhou's history, culture, and peoples include: Corrigan, *Miao Textiles From China*; Jenks, *Insurgency and Social Disorder*; Oakes, *Tourism and Modernity*; Schein, *Minority Rules*; and Wright, *Promise of the Revolution*.

24. The single category "Miao" masks a much more complex reality. For a more detailed discussion of the complexities and political implications of the labels Miao and Hmong, see Schein, *Minority Rules*, xiii-xiv, 3–4. For a discussion of ethnonyms in southwest China under the PRC, see Gladney, *Muslim Chinese*, 302–6. For case studies of the complex process of minority nationality identification for the groups Yi, Naxi, and Zhuang, respectively, see Harrell, "The History of the History of the Yi"; McKhann, "The Naxi and the Nationalities Question"; and Kaup, *Creating the Zhuang*.

25. For a detailed account of Miao migration, see Michaud and Culas, "The Hmong."

26. Victor H. Mair, pers. comm.

27. Gladney, *Muslim Chinese*, 81–87.

28. See, e.g., Link, *Evening Chats in Beijing*, 201–2, note 19.

29. For an overview of earlier Chinese depictions of foreigners, see Hostetler, *Qing Colonial Enterprise*, 87–96.

30. For a full color reproduction and translation into French, see Empereur Kangxi and Jiao Bingzhen, *Le Gengzhitu*.

31. Ledderose, *Ten Thousand Things*, 98–101.

32. An elaborate album for Yunnan painted on silk includes a detailed map at the beginning of each of its four volumes. See "Dian yi tushuo," housed in the Institute of History and Philology, Academia Sinica. An album that covers portions of Guangdong also includes a map of the region whose inhabitants it depicts. See "Lianshanting Lianzhou fen xia Yao pai diyu quantu," housed in the Società Geografica Italiana (Chinese Catalog nos. 62 and 67). "Tai fan tushuo," Fu Ssu-nien Library, Academia Sinica, also includes a map. For a fascinating study of cultural mapping in early modern Japan that includes consideration of both cartography and various genres of literature, see Yonemoto, *Mapping Early Modern Japan*. For a study on how maps, travel writing, and pictures contributed to Taiwan's integration into the Qing empire, see Teng, *Taiwan's Imagined Geography*.

33. Several albums I have seen do not include any text. The texts were almost certainly discarded when albums were rebound by those who had acquired them on the foreign art market, could not read them, and did not value the calligraphy or the ethnographic content.

34. A small number of albums for other provinces are organized by activity rather than by ethnic group, but they are the exception. See, e.g., Musée Guimet 32229. A number of pages from this album are reproduced in Lombard-Salmon, *Un exemple d'acculturation chinoise*.

35. Ledderose, *Ten Thousand Things*, chap. 7.

36. Ibid., 170.

37. Ibid., 175.

38. This album is unusual in more than one way; Hua Gelao is not one of the eighty-two standard ethnonyms commonly found in the albums for Guizhou.

39. For example, a later album, housed in the Società Geografica Italiana (Chinese Catalog no. 60) departs in many instances from the standard tropes. See Hostetler, *Qing Colonial Enterprise*, chap. 7.

40. For a more detailed discussion of the hairstyle variations in the illustrations of the Madeng (Stirrup) Longjia (fig. 11), see Hostetler, "Chinese Ethnography," 123–26.

41. The only case of identical albums I have seen is a rare instance of a color album printed by woodblock. Copies are housed in the Guizhou Provincial Museum, and the Library of the Central Nationalities Institute, Beijing, under the titles "Guizhou Miaozu tu," and "Miaozu fengsu tushuo" respectively. The latter album is incomplete.

42. For a complete listing of those viewed by the author, see the Appendix to Hostetler, *Qing Colonial Enterprise*. The National Museum of Natural History in Beijing also contains numerous albums to which I have not had access.

43. Edkins, "Miau Tsi Tribes," vol. 2, 74.

44. For a full summary of this scholarship, see Hostetler, *Qing Colonial Enterprise*. For a more recent exhibit catalog that includes discussion of the albums in the collection of the Società Geografica Italiana (in both Italian and English), see *Carte di riso*.

45. Tian, *Yanjiao jiwen*. These findings are based on research carried out for Guizhou. They are only meant to be illustrative, not comprehensive for all of southwest China.

46. The earlier *Qian ji* was by Guo Zizhang, the later by Li Zongfang.

47. This is not to say that the information thus obtained was purely "objective." Inquiry and interpretation is always shaped to some degree by the interests and experience of the ethnographer. The *Qing Imperial Illustrations of Tributary Peoples* describes forty-two groups for Guizhou. The 1834 text, like that of a handful of albums, is significantly curtailed. This may reflect a reduced interest in ethnographic detail by the nineteenth century. For a fuller analysis of the development of ethnographic writing in Guizhou over this time span, see Hostetler, *Qing Colonial Enterprise*, chap. 5.

48. Ethnographic studies on the Yi groups referred to as Luoluo in the Miao albums include: Harrell, *Perspectives on the Yi*; Harrell, *Ways of Being Ethnic*; Harrell, Bamo, and Ma, *Mountain Patterns*; Mueggler, *The Age of Wild Ghosts*; and Oppitz and Hsu, *Naxi and Moso Ethnography*. As these studies reveal, the term Yi masks significant ethnic and cultural complexity.

49. On the cultural need for stereotyping, see Gilman, "Introduction."

50. As Susan Blum describes in *Portraits of "Primitives,"* a similar variety of factors, even today, goes into ascribing traits to minority groups within China. Part Two of her book describes this contemporary process of characterization for various minorities in Yunnan. A consequence, if not a primary purpose, of this type of cultural mapping of "others" was the corollary creation of a Han identity. For more on the civilizing projects, and on the importance of majority-minority relationships to

identity, see Cheung, *Appropriating Alterity*; Gladney, *Making Majorities*; Gladney, "Representing Nationality in China"; Hansen, *Lessons in Being Chinese*; and Harrell, *Cultural Encounters*.

51. For works on ethnic consciousness prior to the modern era, see Crossley, *A Translucent Mirror*; and Elliott, *The Manchu Way*. Edward Rhoads' *Manchus and Han* addresses issues of Han and Manchu ethnicity somewhat later, in the transition period from dynastic to republican China.

52. Watson and Rawski, *Death Ritual*. Han interest in minority culture in China is still largely determined by many of these same categories. See Blum, *Portraits of "Primitives*," esp. 76–88.

53. Fascination with sexuality, prompted by different sets of expectations regarding courtship, marriage, and family life, *is* a recurring theme in mainstream representations of minority groups in China. See, e.g., Diamond, "Defining the Miao," esp. 102–4; Gladney, "Representing Nationality in China"; Harrell, "Civilizing Projects," esp. 10–13; Schein, *Minority Rules*; and Schein, "Gender and Internal Orientalism."

54. Watson, "Structure of Chinese Funerary Rites," 3. In Watson's analysis, the importance of correct ritual practice (orthopraxy) is more important in China than correct doctrine (orthodoxy), thus leaving open the possibility for greater diversity in Chinese religious beliefs than in actual practices. Watson also outlines a sequence of nine standardized rites, 12–15. See also Rawski, "A Historian's Approach," and the other chapters in the same volume.

55. This still applies today. See Blum, *Portraits of "Primitives*," 79–80.

56. For further discussion on orientalism, see note 1.

57. For Japan, see Bremen and Shimizu, *Anthropology and Colonialism in Asia*, that examines Dutch and Japanese ethnography in the colonial context; and Ohnuki-Tierney, "Conceptual Model." For Chinese representations of "Others" during the modern period, see Gladney, "Representing Nationality in China"; Schein, "Gender and Internal Orientalism"; and Schein, *Minority Rules*, esp. chap. 4.

58. See, e.g., McNeill, *Rise of the West*.

59. This same logic has allowed the "non-West" to view racism as something that is uniquely "Western" in origin and practice. For a discussion of the construction of race in China, see Dikötter, *Discourse of Race*.

60. For a critique of the use of the term Western, see Lewis and Wigen, *The Myth of Continents*, chap. 2. They show how the geographical area encompassed by the term has expanded over time to include more and more territory; it now refers to localities that have become "westernized." Because of the ubiquity of the use of "West" and "non-West," I cannot completely escape the use of these terms even while critiquing some of the assumptions they have come to entail. When I use the words "West" or "Western," I refer to Europe and (when pertinent) the United States. When I use these terms to connote more than geographical location, I put them in quotation marks.

61. See Thongchai, *Siam Mapped*, for a ground-breaking description of this process in Siam.

62. For more on Japanese expansion during this period, see Walker, *Conquest of Ainu Lands*.

63. Sasaki, "*Ainu-e*: A Historical Review."

64. Howell, "Ainu and the Early Modern Japanese State," 97–98.

65. This is reminiscent of the ambivalence that surrounded tributary relationships with the Qing. Many peoples who were represented in the *Imperial Illustrations of Tributary Peoples*—including Europeans—would not have acknowledged tributary relationships with the Qing. For analogous ambiguities surrounding relationships between the Qing Emperors and the Dalai Lama, see Hevia, "Lamas, Emperors, and Rituals."

66. For more on the relationship between the Ainu and state power in the early modern period, see Siddle, *Race, Resistance and the Ainu*, chap. 2.

67. Ezo can refer either to the island of Hokkaido or to its residents.

68. Whether the earliest edition of this gazetteer contained the illustrated appendix is open to question. Later editions most definitely did. See Sasaki, "*Ainu-e*: A Historical Review," 82.

69. Sasaki, "On *Ainu-e*," 221, reproduces an illustration from the *Ezo-shi*.

70. I have consulted the copy of the *Ezo-shi* in the collection of the University Museum at the University of Pennsylvania.

71. For a full black-and-white reproduction of a hand scroll housed in the Hamburg Museum of Ethnography that bears the title *Ezo-shima kikan* (Strange views from the Island of [the] Ezo), see Prunner, "Ainu Scroll." The title of a four-volume printed work in the library of the Museum of Ethnography in Rotterdam—*Illustrations and Descriptions of the Northern Ainu*—includes the same two Chinese characters often found in the suffix to Miao albums. Pronounced *tu shuo* in Chinese, the expression literally means "illustrations and explanations." Later series of paintings with varied content, by Teiryo Kodama, were entitled *Ezo Customs and Manners*. Shimanojo Murakami (1760–1808), who had firsthand access to Ainu people in his position as a shogunate official in Ezo, authored *Curious Sights of Ezo Island* (Ezo-shima kikan) in 1799. According to Sasaki, it "offers the most extensive description of Ainu Culture and Society presented in the *Ainu-e* format." Sasaki, "*Ainu-e*: A Historical Review," 84.

72. For a "List of the Old Japanese-written Documents on Ezo 1681–1868," see Kodama, *Ainu Historical*, 283–85. For a full discussion of artists of *Ainu-e*, see Sasaki, "*Ainu-e*: A Historical Review"; Sasaki, "On *Ainu-e*"; and MacRitchie, *The Aïnos*. The best reproductions of *Ainu-e* are found in the 1991 exhibit catalog *Kakizaki Hakyo to sono jidai*, Hokkaidoritsu Hakodate Bijutsukan.

73. Prunner, "Ainu Scroll," 230. See also Siddle, *Race, Resistance and the Ainu*, 44.

74. Hakyo Kakizaki painted a series that goes by this title in 1783. See Sasaki, "On *Ainu-e*," 223, for a reproduction.

75. Sasaki, "*Ainu-e*: A Historical Review," 84.

76. A recent, best-selling historical novel whose tension centers around these themes is Orhan Pamuk's *My Name is Red*.

77. Rogers, "Itineraries and Town Views," vol. 2, book 1.

78. *Süleymānnāme*, History of Sultan Süleyman, 1558. Topkapi Sarayi Muzesi. Süleyman reigned for another eight years after the appearance of the book.

79. The images are reproduced in *Topkapi à Versailles*, 325–26. The original is housed in the Topkapi Sarayi Muzesi.

80. Ms. Arab 6074–6077. These particular albums contain an assortment of

album leaves, only some of which fit the above description. Other album leaves would appear to have come from illuminated manuscripts depicting famous stories. How they came to be in the collection of the Bibliothèque nationale is unknown. It would seem that they might have been purchased separately, and then rebound into the existing albums. Each page of the album is bordered in marbled paper. The fact that the illustrations may have been rebound at a later date raises the question of whether any of these illustrations may have, at one time, been accompanied by (additional) text. For further description see *Revue des Bibliothèques*, 167–76.

81. "Figures naturelles de Turquie, par Raynal," 1688. The original is housed in the Bibliothèque nationale, Département des Estampes, Od 7. This manuscript is described in *Topkapi à Versailles*, 113.

82. "Costumes turcs de la Cour et de la ville de Constantinople en 1720, peints en Turquie, par un artiste turc," Bibliothèque nationale, Département des Estampes, Od 6. This manuscript is also described in *Topkapi à Versailles*, 114.

83. The oldest are entitled "Costumes de la Cour du Grand Seigneur" and are dated 1600 and 1630 respectively. Both works are illustrated, with annotations on separate pages. The earlier work is in French, the later in Italian. The latter includes peoples of various national origins including Moors, Greeks, Armenians, and Turks, to name a few. People of various professions are also depicted, such as vendors. Women are portrayed as well. Bibliothèque nationale, Département des Estampes, Od 3 and Od 5.

84. This same process can be traced in European inquiry into China during roughly the same period. Joachim Bouvet, a Jesuit missionary to China, published a work in 1697 entitled *L'Etat présent de la Chine en figures* that included a series of illustrations of Chinese figures hardly representative of the "present state" of China.

85. Two different catalogs date the albums in the Arabic manuscript collection variously as beginning from 1590, and from the seventeenth century.

A Miao Album
of Guizhou Province

猓玀一

昔年濟火長南夷蔓衍羅羅偏
水西地屬鬼方人信鬼蠻文蚓結
總無稽

猓玀本盧鹿訛為今稱在大定府
屬有黑白二種黑為大姓人皆長身黑
面深目鈎鼻雜髮留髻以青布為襄
籠髮其中束於額若角狀短衣大袖
俗尚鬼故又名羅鬼有文字好畜善
馬習射獵蜀漢時有濟火者從武侯
破孟獲有功封羅甸國王即水西安
氏遠祖也

1. Luoluo

In former years Ji Huo[1] nurtured the southern tribes;
The numerous Luoluo spread out to fill Shuixi.[2]
In the region of ghosts, people believed in ghosts.
Their barbarous script is odd as the earthworm knot.

The Luoluo were originally called Lulu, but their name became erroneously transformed. They are located in Dading Prefecture and are of two kinds, Black and White. The Black, tall with black faces, set-in eyes, and aquiline noses, are the headmen. They shave part of the hair on their heads, but wear beards. They use a dark-colored cloth to wrap up their hair.[3] Some bind it to their forehead in the shape of a horn. They wear short tunics with long sleeves. It is their custom to believe in ghosts, so they are also called "Luo Ghosts." They have their own written language, like livestock, are good with horses, and are practiced in shooting. During Shu Han,[4] Ji Huo followed Zhuge Liang[5] to attack Meng Huo[6] and rendered great service. He was therefore offered the kingship of Luo Dian.[7] He is considered a distant ancestor of the An family in Shuixi.[8]

---

1. According to legend, when Zhuge Liang (181–234 C.E.) was conquering the south, Ji Huo (of the Yi ethnic group) collected grain and cleared trails in northwest Guizhou to help capture the enemy Meng Huo. As a reward, Ji Huo was made King of Luo Dian and ruled the area, whose later residents believed he was their ancestor.

2. Unless otherwise indicated, all place names are in Guizhou.

3. *Qing* is literally "a color of nature," and can mean blue, black, or green. Because of this ambiguity, *qing* is translated here as "dark-colored," or simply "dark."

4. Shu Han (221–263 C.E.), sometimes called the "Minor Han dynasty," or simply Shu, was one of the three kingdoms of the Three Kingdoms period (220–280 C.E.).

5. Zhuge Liang (181–234 C.E.) was chancellor of Shu.

6. Meng Huo was a Yi headman, born in Qujing County, Yunnan. After the death of Liu Bei (162–223 C.E.), King of the Shu, Meng Huo rebelled against the kingdom's new leaders. Zhuge Liang captured and freed Meng Huo seven times, and finally Meng Huo pledged allegiance to the state of Shu.

7. Luo Dian (domain of the Luo) in Guizhou was controlled by the Luoluo.

8. For more on Luoluo history, see Lin, "The Miao-man Peoples," esp. 272–74.

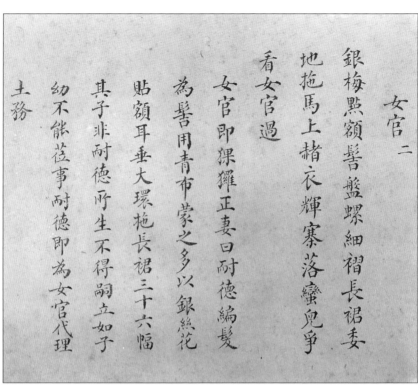

女官 二

銀梅點額髻盤螺細褶長裙委
地拖馬上赭衣輝寨落蠻兒爭
看女官過

女官即猓玀正妻曰耐德編髮
為髻用青布蒙之多以銀絲花
貼額耳垂大環拖長裙三十六幅
其子非耐德所生不得嗣立如子
幼不能蒞事耐德即為女官代理
土務

2. Nüguan (Female Official)

Silver flowers dot her forehead. Her hair plaited,
A finely-pleated long skirt trailing on the ground,
Mounted, in red, a bright contrast to the stockade;
Barbarian sons strive to see Nüguan pass by.

Nüguan is the principal wife of the Luoluo [Chief]. She is called *Naide*, "Patient and Virtuous."[9] Her hair is plaited, bound up, and covered with a dark cloth. She often affixes silver-colored silk flowers to her forehead, and she wears big earrings. Her long skirts contain thirty-six pleats. Only sons born to this wife may be crowned. If her son is too young to assume office, she will act as a female official and be in charge of all affairs.

---

9. *Naide* may simply be a Chinese transliteration of an indigenous term. Whether or not the indigenous term carried the meaning "patient and virtuous," is uncertain. In any case, the Chinese characters conveyed this meaning to the readership of the album.

白猓玀三

猓玀上種黑稱尊白者為卑不
締婚三足釜燃圍坐處茹毛飲血
古風存
白猓玀大定安順皆有之與黑猓
玀同而為下姓無論鼠雀蚯蛻蟲
動之物攫而燔之飲食無盤盂以
三足釜攢食若嵒死則以牛馬革
裏而焚之居普定者為阿和多販
茶為業

3. Bai (White) Luoluo

Among the Luoluo the Black are held in respect.
Humble White may not intermarry with the Black.[10]
Seated around a three-footed pot they cook food.
Munching fur and quaffing blood, old customs survive.

White Luoluo are found in both Dading and Anshun. They belong to the same tribe as the Black Luoluo but are the subordinate clans. They collect and cook any animal that wriggles or moves, including rodents, birds, and insect larvae. This is eaten straight from a three-footed pot; they do not use dishes for eating and drinking. If someone dies of illness, the body is wrapped in skins from cattle or horses and then burned.[11] Those who live in Puding are called "A-he" and many are tea dealers by trade.

---

10. For more on the relationship between the Black Luoluo and the White Luoluo, see Mair, "The Book of Great Deeds."

11. The orthography in this sentence seems to contain an error. Literally it says, "if a pig dies . . . ," however, other album texts on the Bai Luoluo all refer to what happens when a person dies. The character for "pig" is most likely a mis-writing of the word for illness, with which it shares a common radical. It is translated here accordingly, as death ritual for human beings is of primary concern throughout the album.

宋家苗四

襟分長短翦裁新男女冠笄亦
可人卻笑婚姻沿陋俗奪親追逐
禮無因

宋家苗在貴陽本宋裔春秋時為
楚所俘放之南徼即宋宣慰祖也
通漢語男子帽而長襟女子笄而
短襟將嫁婿家往迎女家率親戚
篁楚之謂之奪親旦進盟於姑男
女燂湯以沐三日而罷

4. Songjia Miao

Upper garments, both long and short, are newly trimmed.
Now how pleasing are men and women, capped and pinned.
Heeding rustic customs, their weddings make us laugh.
"Capturing the bride"; a ritual without reason.[12]

Songjia Miao are located in Guiyang. They are the descendants of the Song[13] who were captured by the state of Chu,[14] and banished to the southern border region during the Spring and Autumn period. They were ancestors of the Song pacification office.[15] The Songjia Miao can speak Chinese. Men wear hats and long upper garments. Women wear hairpins and short upper garments. Before a wedding, the bridegroom and his family go to greet the bride, but the bride's family gathers all the relatives together and beats up the bridegroom's family. This custom is called "capturing the bride." In the morning, the girl is offered water for bathing. Both men and women heat water and bathe. After three days it is over.

---

12. Literally, "capturing the bride and following in pursuit are rituals without reason."

13. Song was a kingdom located between Henan, Shandong, and Anhui Provinces, during the Spring and Autumn period (*Chun Qiu*) (770–476 B.C.E.).

14. Chu was a kingdom located in Hubei, Hunan, and parts of neighboring provinces, during the Spring and Autumn period (770–476 B.C.E.).

15. According to Hucker, *Dictionary of Official Titles*, the *Xuanweisi*, which translates as either "pacification office" or "pacification officer," "was one of the most prestigious titles granted to aboriginal tribes in southwestern China and their natural, mostly hereditary chiefs," 251.

蔡家苗五

居喪食粥禮曾諸做戛相沿俗
又憨共說蠻妝看不得尺餘高髻
綰長簪

蔡家苗即蔡人春秋時為楚子町
俘貴筑修文清平清鎮大定威寧
平遠皆有之男子製衣短為衣婦人
韝髻緣飾青布高尺許綰以長簪
居喪食稗粥三月殺牛名戚黨吹
笙跳舞名曰做戛翁妁不通言語
夫兊汉婦殉婦家奪去乃免

5. Caijia Miao

Eating gruel in mourning, past ritual still observed.
Long passed on, the zuo ga, *a foolish custom too.*
All say their adornment's not pleasing to the eye
With hair coiled up and pinned more than one foot high.[16]

The Caijia Miao are the same as the Cai people.[17] They were captured by the people of Chu at the time of the Spring and Autumn period.[18] They are found in Guizhu, Xiuwen, Qingping, Qingzhen, Dading, Weining, and Pingyuan. Men wear tunics made of felt. Married women use felt to dress their hair, wearing it more than one foot high. They decorate it with dark cloth and bind it up with a hairpin. When in mourning, the Caijia Miao eat gruel made from grasses. In the third month they slaughter cattle and invite relatives and friends to play the mouth organ[19] and dance together. This festival is called *zuo ga*. Within the family, the father and daughter-in-law must never talk to each other. When the husband dies, the wife is buried alive with him unless her family rescues her.

---

16. Throughout the text, unless the meaning would be significantly altered, *chi*, which is equivalent to one-third of a meter, is translated as "foot."

17. In Chinese, *Cairen*.

18. The Spring and Autumn period dates from 770 to 476 B.C.E.

19. Called a *sheng* in Chinese, this musical instrument consists of reed pipes of varying lengths, each with finger holes.

卡尤犵家六

邑管遷来有卡尤青巾綰髻自
風流如花犵女争途出跳月場中
擲綵毬

卡尤犵家在貴陽平越都勻安
順興義各屬有黄羅班莫柳文
龍等姓五代時楚王馬殷自邑
管遷来衣尚青以帕束首婦女
多繼好長裙細褶多至二十餘
幅孟春跳月結綵毬視所歡者
擲之奔而不禁聘用牛多至三
五十頭

6. Kayou Zhongjia

Once under Yong's control, the Kayou then moved here.[20]
Hair bound up in dark cloth, each shows off his own style.
Like flowers, women strive to show themselves outside.
Dancing on moonlit grounds, they toss a bright-hued ball.

The Kayou Zhongjia are located in Guiyang, Pingyue, Duyun, Anshun, and Xingyi. They have the surnames Huang, Luo, Ban, Mo, Liu, Wen, and Long. During the Five Dynasties period, Ma Yin, King of Chu, immigrated to these areas from the control of Yong.[21] The Kayou like to wear dark garments and bind their heads with kerchiefs. Women, most of whom are slim, favor long, finely-pleated skirts made from as many as twenty or more panels.[22] In early spring, they celebrate the moon-dancing festival. They make colorful balls. If they see someone that pleases them they throw it to him or her, and run off together with their beloved without restriction. For a betrothal gift, they give as many as thirty to fifty head of cattle.

---

20. Yong is the name of a county in Guangxi.

21. The Five Dynasties date from 907 to 960 C.E. and ruled over North China while the Ten Kingdoms (907–979 C.E.) held sway in the south. The kingdom of Chu had its capital at Changsha in present-day Hunan.

22. They may have made the cloth for their skirts on backstrap looms, which only allow for fairly narrow strips of cloth to be woven. If this were the case, they would have needed to sew multiple panels together to make skirts.

補籠狇家七

補籠風俗未相懸狇子分支色
總妍獨怪殘冬風雪裏齊擂銅鼓
賀新年

補籠狇家在定番廣順二州俗與
卞尤同以十二月為歲首擊銅鼓
賀歲掘地得鼓即以為諸葛所遺
富者重賞購之喪則屠牛召戚友
以牛角歡飲醉或致於相殺主人不
食肉惟啖魚蝦既葬以傘覆墓期
而焚之性剽悍出入帶利刀睚眦

7. Bulong (Basket-Repairing) Zhongjia

Bulong customs differ little from the Kayou.
Children of the Zhong, ah, so beautiful they seem.
How odd that in the cruel winter's wind and snow they
Always beat their bronze drums to welcome the New Year.

The Bulong Zhongjia are located in Dingfan and Guangshun Districts. Their customs are similar to those of the Kayou. For them, the New Year begins in the twelfth month.[23] They greet it by striking a bronze drum. When they dig in the ground and find a drum, they consider it to be the legacy of Zhuge Liang.[24] The rich must pay a high price to buy the drum. At funerals, cattle are butchered and dressed, and relatives and friends are invited. Drinking from the "ox horn of happiness,"[25] the guests often get drunk and sometimes even wind up killing each other. The host does not usually eat meat but only fish and shrimp. After burial, the grave is covered by an umbrella. After a certain period of time, it is burned. By nature the Bulong are alert and fierce. When coming and going they carry sharp knives. They will avenge even an angry look.

---

23. The texts of a number of other Miao albums say they celebrate the New Year in the tenth month.

24. Zhuge Liang (181–234 C.E.) was chancellor of Shu.

25. The "ox horn of happiness" is a cup made of ox-horn; two persons usually drink together, using the same cup, to show their friendship.

青狇家八

俗至青夷更不同擲毬善奕習成
風煌煌正朔無由識木刻傳來
是所宗

青狇家在古州清江丹江等處以
青布蒙首衣青衣女子白皙而性
敏工刺繡善奕棋以擲毬為樂所
私者曰馬郎夜輒與之飲父母知
而不禁惟避其兄弟婚姻苟合相
悅者以牛酒致聘不知正朔以木
刻為信

8. Qing (Blue) Zhongjia[26]

The customs of the blue yi are not all alike.[27]
Playing toss, skilled at chess, their ways become gentle.
The resplendent New Year, they do not recognize.
Notching wood as of yore, this is what they honor.

The Qing Zhongjia are located in Guzhou, Qingjiang, and Danjiang. They cover their heads with dark cloth and wear dark garments. The girls are fair complexioned and are clever by nature. They work at embroidery and are skilled at playing chess. For enjoyment, they toss a ball.[28] Those with whom they are intimate are called Malang. As soon as night falls they go off drinking together. The parents know and do not forbid this, but girls must hide it from their brothers. At marriage, those who are pleasing to each other and have had illicit intercourse reach a betrothal agreement involving cattle and wine. They do not observe the calendar, but notch wood to keep records.

---

26. As noted above, *qing* is literally "a color of nature," and can mean blue, black, or green. Because of this ambiguity, I usually translate *qing* as "dark-colored," or simply "dark." However, in instances where *qing* is used as a proper noun, I use "blue" in order to remain stylistically consistent with translations of other names such as Hong (Red) Miao and Bai (White) Miao, as well as to differentiate them from the Hei (Black) Miao. This translation of proper names also avoids possible confusion; *qing* is not a reference to dark skin. The illustrations in most Miao albums depict the Qing Zhongjia and Qing Miao wearing blue and/or black, but not green.

27. *Yi* is a broad term for foreigner or barbarian.

28. This may be an allusion to the same courtship practice described above for the Kayou Zhongjia.

曾竹龍家 九

牽羊負酒重親情自帶新衣博
富名設祭卜期惟七七家人扎尾
莫先塋

曾竹龍家在安順府婦女白衣桶
裙戴細布方巾以髮扎一尾名曰
髮尾豬油擦之遇親戚喜慶事
負酒牽羊以賀而自帶新衣數
龍裳以誇富歿則焚之揀骨而藝每
七月七日祭先塋

9. Cengzhu Longjia

Leading goats, bearing wine, they value family ties.
To make known wealth and fame they bring new clothes to wear.
Divining, sacrificing, on double seven,[29]
Pig-tailed family members make graveside libations.

The Cengzhu Longjia are located in Anshun Prefecture. Women wear white tunics, straight skirts, and kerchiefs made of fine cloth. Using their hair, they fashion a kind of tail, called a "hair-tail," into which they rub lard. When they meet friends and relatives or have a happy occasion, they bring wine and lead goats to celebrate. They also bring several sets of new clothes in order to show off their wealth. When someone dies the body is burned, then the bones are picked up and buried. Every year, on the seventh day of the seventh month, they make sacrifices at the graves of those who have preceded them in death.

---

29. Double seven refers to the seventh day of the seventh month in the Chinese lunar calendar.

狗耳龍家 十

螺髻雙翹狗耳名鬼竿篁處最
關情藥珠妝點斑衣綵笑舞春風
偶自成

狗耳龍家在廣順州康佐司男子
束髮不冠婦人辮髮螺髻上指若
狗耳狀衣衣斑衣以五色藥珠為飾
貧者薏苡代之春時立木於野名
曰鬼竿男女旋躍而擇配既奔女
氏以牛馬贖之方通媒妁

10. Gou'er (Dog-Eared) Longjia

Two spiraled plaits curl upward, hence their name, "dog-eared."
The "ghost pole," set in place, above all concerns love.
Adorned with seed pearls, their speckled garments shimmer.
Laughter, dance, and spring breeze; naturally they find mates.

The Gou'er Longjia are located in Guangshun District and Kangzuo Sub-District. Men bind their hair up, but do not wear hats. Married women wear their hair braided up into spirals that stick up in the shape of dogs' ears. They also wear speckled upper garments, and ornament themselves with five-colored seed pearls.[30] Poor women use the seeds of Job's tears instead of seed pearls. In the spring, the Gou'er Longjia erect a pole in the open. This is called a "ghost pole." Men and women skip and dance around the pole, and select a mate. Only after a couple runs off together and the woman's clan gives cattle and horses to redeem her do they make an agreement through a matchmaker.

---

30. Seed pearls are small, imperfect pearls. The name derives from their irregular shape. The Chinese name translates literally as medicine pearls. This may be because seed pearls were used to make pearl powder for ulcers.

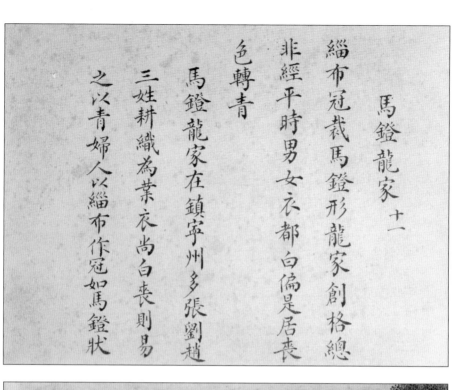

馬鐙龍家十一

緇布冠裁馬鐙形龍家創格總
非經平時男女衣都白偏是居喪
色轉青
馬鐙龍家在鎮寧州多張劉趙
三姓耕織為業衣尚白喪則易
之以青婦人以緇布作冠如馬鐙狀

11. Madeng (Stirrup) Longjia

Cut-out caps of black cloth in the shape of stirrups,
Devised by the Longjia, how unconventional!
Ordinarily men and women wear white clothes.
When in mourning, conversely, the color turns dark.

The Madeng Longjia are located in Zhenning District. Most of them bear the surnames Zhang, Liu, and Zhao. They are farmers and weavers by trade. They favor white clothing, but when in mourning change into a dark color. Married women use black silk cloth to make stirrup-shaped caps.

龍家之類雜吾州此種緣何號大
頭祇為絲螺盤若盍殊名儕輩
詭無由
大頭龍家在鎮寧州及普定男子
帶竹笠婦人青衣短裙斂馬髮
於髮盤髻如盍故大頭名云以

大頭龍家十二

12. Datou (Large-Headed) Longjia

Different types of Longjia scattered through our district,
Why is it that this kind has the name "Large-Headed?"
It's just that coiled up, their hair's like a cover.
Each sort has its own name. Is this without reason?

The Datou Longjia are located in Zhenning District, and in Puding. Men wear conical grass or bamboo hats, and women dress in dark tunics and short skirts. They collect hair from the manes of horses to coil up with their own hair to build it up high.[31] That is why they are called "Large-Headed."

---

31. Some albums depict the Datou Longjia as having truly big hair.

花苗

曉妝插得木梳新斑駁花衣繫
裹身吹動蘆笙鈴響叶陌頭跳
月女懷春

花苗在貴陽大定遵義廳屬
以六月為歲首男子首纏青布
緝敗布帶為衣婦人斂馬髮尾
為大䯻插木梳於上花衣綵袖
孟春跳月男吹蘆笙女振響鈴
歌謔終日暮挈所私而歸莖不
用棺斂手足而瘞之下地擲雞

13. Hua (Flowery) Miao

Dressing at dawn, she inserts a new wooden comb
And wraps colorful clothing around her body.
Blowing reeds, shaking bells—sound, movement, harmonize.[32]
Strangers dance in moonlight. Young girls cherish springtime.

The Hua Miao are under the jurisdiction of Guiyang, Dading, and Zunyi. They regard the sixth month as the beginning of the year. The men wrap their heads with dark cloth and join together pieces of old and worn out cloth, wearing this for tunics. Married women gather hair from horses' manes and tails to plait together with their own hair, sticking a wooden comb into the top. They wear colorful tunics with variegated sleeves. In the first month of spring they dance under the moon. Men play the mouth organ[33] and women shake musical bells. They sing and jest the whole day. In the evening they lead the one they want for themselves home with them. When it comes to burial they do not use coffins. They arrange the hands and feet, and simply inter the corpse. They divine the place by throwing a chicken.

---

32. This is an elliptical reference to the moon dance at which Hua Miao women shake hand bells while men play the mouth organ.

33. *Lüsheng.*

紅苗十四

斑絲織就彩衣新夏五逢寅是忌

辰見說婦人能解鬥紅苗雖悍豈

難馴

紅苗在銅仁府有吳龍石麻白五姓

衣用斑絲織成牲畜皆掊殺以火

去毛微煮帶血而食人死將遺衣

裝其形像擊鼓歌舞名曰調鼓

五月寅日夫婦異寢不敢言亦不

出戶以避鬼且忌虎也每類相鬥

必婦人勸方解同

14. Hong (Red) Miao

Colored silk now woven, their brilliant clothes are new.
During the fifth month they observe a taboo day.
Appearing and speaking, women can break up fights.
Though cruel, can the Red Miao be difficult to tame?

The Hong Miao are located in Tongren Prefecture. They have five surnames: Wu, Long, Shi, Ma, and Bai. Their tunics are of woven variegated silk. As domestic animals are fattened they are culled. Using fire
to remove the hair, they cook the meat only slightly and eat it while it
is still bloody. When a person dies, they take some of the clothing that
person has left and use it to dress up an effigy. They strike a drum,
sing, and dance. This is called harmonizing with the drum. On their
taboo day during the fifth month, husband and wife sleep separately.
In order to avoid ghosts as well as tigers they do not dare to speak and
do not leave their dwellings. Each subgroup fights among itself. It is
necessary for the women to exhort them to relent.

白苗

飼牛供祀最殷勤牯牽來勝
負兮誰是老成應主祭白衣青
套束腰裙

白苗貴定龍里黔西皆有之衣
白衣男子科頭跣足婦人藍髻
長簪跳月之習與花苗同祀祖
擇大犄牛飼之既壯乃聚合寨
之牛鬥於野勝者吉卜期屠之
主祭者白衣青套細摺長裙祭
畢合親族歌飲為歡

15. Bai (White) Miao

Most attentively they raise beef for sacrifice.
Fighting bulls are led forth for vict'ry or defeat.
A venerable one must lead the sacrifice
With white top, dark wrap, and a skirt tied at the waist.

Bai Miao are found in Guiding, Longli, and Qianxi. They wear white tunics. Men wear their hair in a topknot with no hat, and go barefoot. Married women coil up their hair using long hairpins. They have the same custom of "moon dancing" as the Flowery Miao. To offer sacrifices to ancestors, they select big bulls to raise. When the village's bulls are robust, they gather them together and watch them fight in a field. The winning bull is considered auspicious. A time is divined for its slaughter. The one who leads the sacrifice wears a white tunic, a dark outer garment, and a finely-pleated long skirt. After the ceremony, the relatives and clansmen sing, drink, and dance for joy.

女工課績編漚麻一幅青巾倣九

華膌後髮垂婚事畢芒鞋竹笠

稱田家

青苗在貴筑黔西修文平越鎮

寧等處衣尚青婦人以青布蒙

首製衣如九華巾麻衣皆其自

織男子竹笠草履未婚者翦膌

後髮娶乃留之性強悍出入必

佩刀

16. Qing (Blue) Miao

Women work at spinning thread wholly from soaked hemp.
One dark-colored kerchief resembles nine flowers.
If hair hangs down behind, marriage has taken place.
Straw sandals, bamboo hats; they could be called peasants.

Qing Miao are located in Guizhu, Qianxi, Xiuwen, Pingyue, and Zhenning. They favor a dark color for their tunics. Women cover their heads with dark cloth constructed like a "nine flower" kerchief. Their hempen tunics are all of their own weaving. Men wear conical grass or bamboo hats, and straw sandals. Those who are unmarried cut their hair in the back. After marriage they let it grow. Their nature is strong and fierce. When they come and go they always wear knives at their waists.

臭腐始告釭成日醋菜珍為異味

獸一切蠕動之物雜貯甕中俟蜋蛆

野蔬艱於鹽以蕨灰代之得死鳥

婦人短衣花袖額束銀勒食糯飯

項圈耳環跣足陟岡巑捷若猿猴

尚黑頭標白羽男女皆梳髻插簪

黑苗八寨丹江清江古州皆有之衣

新妝

嘗依水傍山名各異齊施銀勒鬥

蕨灰漬水野蔬香醋菜釭成好共

17. Hei (Black) Miao

Bracken ash, pure water, fragrant wild vegetables,
And fermented foods; they are fond of all of these.
By water or in the mountains, their names differ.[34]
All sporting silver chain, they vie in adornment.

Hei Miao are found in Bazhai, Danjiang, Qingjiang, and Guzhou. They favor black tunics. White feathers top their heads. Both men and women comb their hair up, use hairpins, and wear neck-rings and ear-rings. Barefoot, they climb mountains as nimbly as monkeys. Married women wear short tunics with colorful sleeves, and bind their foreheads with a silver bridle. The Hei Miao eat glutinous rice and wild vegetation. It is so hard for them to get salt that they use bracken ash instead. Whenever they get dead birds, wild animals, or any kind of wriggling animal, they put them into earthen jars. Only when rotten and full of maggots is it ready to serve. Called *yin cai*, this dish is valued for its unusual flavor.

---

34. *Ming*, translated here as "name," refers to the names of the different subdivisions within the Hei Miao rather than to given names (or surnames). Varieties of Hei Miao include Bazhai Hei Miao, Qingjiang Hei Miao, Louju Hei Miao, Hei Shan Miao, and Hei Sheng Miao. See Hostetler, *Qing Colonial Enterprise*, 139.

東苗十八

只留頂上髮氉氉明月圓時享

祀譜少婦花衣多缺袖一生露臂

又何堪

東苗在貴筑龍里清平有族無姓

婦人花衣無袖以兩幅遮前覆後

著細摺短裙男子留頂髮短衣背

甲中秋延鬼師祭祖及親族亡故

者屠牛陳肴饌循序而呼之祭畢

酣歌劇飲每春獵於山獲禽鳥

亦必荐祖

18. Dong (East) Miao

They let their hair grow out on top. It's thin and long.
When the moon is full they perform sacrifices.
Most young married women's colorful tops lack sleeves.
How can they bear a whole lifetime with arms exposed?

Dong Miao are located in Guizhu, Longli, and Qingping. They have clans, but not surnames. Married women wear colorful tunics without sleeves. The garments are made of two panels of cloth, one covering the breast and another covering the back. They also wear finely pleated short skirts. Men grow their hair, wearing it up on top of their heads. They wear short tunics and vests. At the Mid-Autumn Festival, the Dong Miao engage a ghost master to offer sacrifices to their ancestors. When a relative dies they slaughter a water buffalo, spread out the sacrificial meat in an orderly manner, and call out to the departed. After the sacrifice, people sing merrily and drink heavily. Every spring, the Dong Miao hunt in the mountains. They must sacrificially offer to their ancestors the birds and beasts they capture.

早築霜場合牡牛爭延善祝賽
豐收童男少女齊拖彩學步吹笙
舞不休
西苗在平越清平有謝馬何羅盧
雷等姓衣尚青以青布纏首白布
裹腿婦人盤髻插梳秋收後合牡
牛於野祝者鐘衣鐘帽皮靴腰圓
細摺裙童男女青衣綵帶吹笙舞
蹈隨之歷三晝夜乃殺牛以賽豐
年名曰祭白虎除夕置雞酒呼合

38   A Miao Album of Guizhou Province

19. Xi (West) Miao

Early on, the frosty field's prepared for the bull.
To keep blessings, they offer thanks for a rich yield.
Lads and lasses alike dress in brilliant colors.
Learning steps, playing pipes, they dance without ceasing.

Xi Miao are located in Pingyue and Qingping. They have the surnames Xie, Ma, He, Luo, Lu, and Lei. They favor dark clothing, bind their heads with dark cloth, and wrap their legs with white cloth. Married women coil up their hair and stick a comb into it. After the autumn harvest, the Xi Miao accompany a sturdy bull to an uncultivated area. The one who performs the blessing wears felt garments and a felt hat, along with leather boots, and a finely-pleated skirt around the waist. Male and female youths, wearing dark garments and colorful belts, blow on reed-pipes and dance. This continues for three days and nights, whereupon they slaughter the bull to celebrate the abundant harvest. It is called offering sacrifices to the White Tiger. On the eve of the New Year the Xi Miao prepare a feast of chicken and wine and call [people] together.

天苗二十

摽梅時節慮蹉跎卞聽笙簧意若
何莫道秦樓多寂寞來鸞蕭史
夜來過

天苗亦名天家多姬姓在平越州
青衣左袵男子緝木葉為上衣下
穿短裙女子年十五六即構竹樓野
處未婚者吹竹笙誘之成配以十一
月為大節婦人工織善染人死用
籐蔓束之樹間任風雨化之

20. Yao Miao

The plum will fall when ripe; don't let the chance slip by.
Listening for reed pipes, what are her sentiments?
Don't say that her room is still and solitary;
Xiao Shi,[35] on his phoenix, has come to pass the night.

Yao Miao are also called Yaojia. They are located in Pingyue. Most of them have Ji for a surname. They wear dark jackets that fasten on the left. Men fasten leaves together to make tunics, and wear short skirts. Girls, upon reaching the age of fifteen or sixteen *sui*,[36] usually build bamboo structures in the fields. Unmarried men come to play bamboo pipes to induce them into making a match. The eleventh month is an important time for the Yao Miao. Married women are skilled at weaving and dyeing [cloth]. When someone dies, the body is bound up in a tree with rattan. They allow the wind and rain to transform it.

---

35. Xiao Shi is a legendary god good at playing the flute and able to sound like a phoenix. He married the daughter of a duke of the Qin kingdom.

36. Fifteen or sixteen *sui* is equivalent to roughly thirteen to fifteen years old. In Qing China, a child was considered to be one *sui* at birth, and one additional *sui* with every passing Chinese New Year.

獞苗二十一

獞家風俗漸還淳
漢人何事女妝終不改短襦細裙
覆花巾
獞苗在貞豐州自粵西改隸黔
省男子薙髮衣冠俱效漢人女
短衣長裙首蒙花布尚循苗俗
性獷悍嗜殺

21. Nong (Agricultural) Miao

Nongjia customs slowly come round to what is pure.
In hairstyle, dress, and headgear they are like the Han.
How is it that the women's styles still have not changed?
Short jackets, fine pleats, topped with a colorful scarf.

The Nong Miao are located in Zhenfeng District, which once belonged
to Guangxi, but later became part of Guizhou Province. Men shave their
heads and dress just like Han people.[37] Women wear short tunics and
long skirts, and cover their heads with colorful scarves. They still follow Miao customs. Their nature is fierce and cruel; they enjoy killing.

---

37. The translation "Han people" here is literal (*hanren*). While the term *hanzu*,
meaning Han ethnicity, did not come into usage until later, the term *hanren* appears
with some regularity in eighteenth- and early nineteenth-century texts.

打牙仡佬二十二

桶裙無摺織青羊最是夫家不

忍妨新婦一齊齦齒笑打牙風

俗太荒唐

打牙仡佬在平越黔西等州女

子織青羊毛為布以一幅橫圍

腰間謂之桶裙將嫁必打去門

牙二齒恐妨害夫家昕謂齹齒

之民也又翦前髮而披後髮取

齊眉之意

44　　A Miao Album of Guizhou Province

22. Daya (Teeth-Breaking) Gelao

Bucket skirts without pleats are woven from black wool.
Quite rightly the groom's house will not stand for trouble.
Without exception all new brides have toothless smiles.
The custom of breaking teeth is going to excess!

The Daya Gelao are located in Pingyue and Qianxi Districts. Women weave cloth from black wool. They dress in a width of wool worn around the waist, called a "bucket skirt." Before a woman marries, her two front teeth must be knocked out because of a fear that she could bring trouble to the groom's family. These are the so-called "chiseling teeth" people. They also cut bangs in front, but let the hair in back grow long. This hair style signifies that the husband and wife will remain a devoted couple to the end of their days.[38]

---

38. *Qimei* is a play on words. Literally meaning "even with the eyebrows," that is, bangs, the compound also carried the meaning of a married couple. It is not clear from the text whether the play on words comes from the Daya Gelao themselves (i.e., they do it for that reason) or originates with the author of the text.

犷兜苗二十三

到處呼羣射獵詳犷兜女子髻
偏斜短衣無領何須飾蠮蠩䯀
䯀號海巴

犷兜苗鎮逺施秉黃平皆有之
好獵類土人女子偏髻插梳短
衣無領裙不過膝繡五色於胸
袖間以海巴綴蕑為飾䯀如
貫珠其藥箭傷人立殞然不
為盗

23. Gedou Miao

Far and wide cries abound; the clamor of the hunt.
Dressed hair of Gelao women perches toward one side.
With collarless short tops how do they get dressed up?
They string together silkworm cocoons called haiba.[39]

The Gedou Miao are found in Zhenyuan, Shibing, and Huangping. They are as good at hunting as the Turen.[40] Women wear their hair up, inclined toward one side, with a comb inserted. Their short tunics are collarless, and their skirts do not reach beyond the knee. They embroider in five colors on the bust and the sleeves, and ornament themselves with seashells [shaped] like silkworm cocoons, stringing them together like real pearls. If a man is injured by one of their poisoned arrows he will die immediately. They are not, however, given to thievery.

---

39. *Haiba* translates loosely as "seashells."
40. The Turen are another ethnic group; see figure 33 below.

猪屎犵狫 二十四

食獸如狼氣自雄 往来佩劍又
彎弓清平約束遵守不但中
華語漸通

猪屎犵狫在黎平古州石阡等
處身面經年不洗所居穢臭不
堪與犬豕同牢得獸咋食如狼男
子出入必佩刀弩有仇必報如不及
則備牛酒以款有力者片肉卮酒
亦捐軀與之在清平者頗通漢
語聽約束

24. Zhushi (Pig-Filth) Gelao[41]

Wolfing their meat, they exhibit an inbred strength.
Swords and drawn bows at the ready, they come and go.
Those in Qingping are restrained and observe the law,
Learning not only manners,[42] but slowly our speech.

The Zhushi Gelao are located in Liping, Guzhou, and Shiqian. During the course of a full year they never wash their bodies or faces. Their dwellings are unbearably dirty and smelly; they live together in the same sheds as their dogs and pigs. When they catch animals, they gnaw them noisily just like a wolf would. The males carry swords and crossbows whenever they go out. If they have an enemy they will certainly take revenge. If they are not equal to [the task] they will prepare meat and wine to treat someone with strength. For a slice of meat and a cup of wine, they become involved, even to the point of sacrificing their lives. Those in Qingping understand the Chinese language and are able to comply with agreements.[43]

---

41. The second character in the compound *zhushi* translated here as "pig-filth" also carries the more specific meaning of "excrement" or "shit."

42. The grammatical structure here, coupled with the rhythm of the poem, indicates "*zhong hua*" is a verb-object construction rather than a noun. Therefore I do not translate it as "China," but rather choose the word "manners," which approximates a literal translation of "attaining splendor"; manners being a marker of what is (however subjectively) culturally refined.

43. Presumably this refers to agreements made with representatives of the Qing.

犭狫 二十五

高駕羊樓結構新層層遮益綠
杉勺腰圓幅布分名色青白花紅
各有倫
犭狫呼在多有其種不一男女腰
圓幅布名曰桶裙花布曰花犭狫
紅布曰紅犭狫各有族類不通婚
姻死斂以棺而不葬置巖穴間或
臨大河樹木主曰家親殿屋宇去
地數尺駕以巨木上覆杉葉謂之
羊樓

25. Gelao

High up they perch—the yang lou's[44] *roof beams newly joined—*
Hidden and protected by layer on layer of firs,
Waists encircled by cloths the color of their names:
Blue, White, Flowery, Red. Each has its proper place.

The Gelao are found in many localities, and there are different varieties. Men and women both encircle their waists with a panel of cloth called a "bucket-skirt." Those who use variegated cloth are called Flowery Gelao; those who use red are called Red Gelao. Each group has their own tribe and clan. They do not intermarry. When someone dies they arrange the body into a coffin, but do not bury it. Rather they place it in a cave, or in a forest near a river. They call this place *Jia qin dian*, the Temple of the Family. When they construct a house, they remove the earth to a depth of several feet and then, using huge trunks, erect the house, covering the roof with boughs of fir. This kind of building is called a *yang lou*.

---

44. *Yang lou* translates literally as sheep building. I do not use a literal translation because the derivation of the name may be based on the sound of the indigenous word for the structure, rather than any relationship to sheep.

六種苗 二十六

土風歲首奉槃瓠洞狄狑狪

別類呼祭罷幾番連袂舞羅

敢誰說尚無夫

狑狪獞猺狪六種雜居荔

波縣服衣雖別風俗略同歲

首祀奉槃瓠男女連袂歌舞

相悅者負之而去遂婚媾焉

26. Liuzhong (Six Kinds of) Miao

By custom New Year's offerings are made to Pan Hu.[45]
Tho' Dong, Shui, Ling, and Yang are called by different names,
After the sacrifice, some will join sleeves and dance.
Nets are plentiful; who says she still has no man?

Six different kinds of Miao—Shui, Ling, Yang, Zhuang, Yao, and Dong—all live together in Libo County. Although they dress differently their customs are similar. At New Year's they make offerings to Pan Hu. Those who delight in each other go off together, the man carrying the woman away on his back. Then they are married.

---

45. Pan Hu is a mythical dog figure who, along with a Chinese princess, is considered the progenitor of many of China's southern minority groups. For more on Pan Hu, see the entry in Kaltenmark, *Dictionnaire des mythologies*, 159–61; and Birrell, *Chinese Mythology*, 118–20, 264. The Pan Hu myth is also recounted in Litzinger, *Other Chinas*, 58.

水犵狫 二十七

水犵狫真善捕魚入淵信手百
無虛祗孀婦女循苗飾細褶長
裙俗未除

水犵狫在餘慶鎮遠施秉等
慶一名擾家土民稱湯楊龍
者即其老戶善捕魚雖隆冬
亦能入淵男子衣服與漢人同
惟婦女穿細褶裙猶沿苗俗

54   A Miao Album of Guizhou Province

27. Shui (Water) Gelao

Truly the Shui Gelao are skilled at catching fish.
In the deep, one hundred trusty hands. None empty.
Women of all stations adhere to Miao fashion;
Long, finely-pleated skirts have not yet disappeared.

The Shui Gelao are found in Yuqing, Zhenyuan, and Shibing. Another name for them is Raojia Tumin.[46] Those with the surnames Tang, Yang, and Long are respected among them.[47] They are good at catching fish and enter the deep even in the cold of winter. The clothes of the men are like those of the Han Chinese, but the women wear finely-pleated skirts, still conserving Miao custom.

---

46. *Rao* bears the related but contrary meanings of "to disturb, annoy, give trouble" and "docile," or "to train to obedience." *Jia*, the character for "family," forms the suffix for a number of names of minority groups. *Tumin* refers to local peoples, *min* connoting subjects who recognize the authority of the reigning dynasty.

47. An alternate, more literal, translation would be: "Those with the surnames Tang, Yang, and Long are the original families."

鍋圈犵狫二十八

鍋圈又換犵苗妝俗尚斜文課織

忙麵塑虎頭披綵線簸箕托出禮

空王

鍋圈犵狫在平遠州男子以葛織

斜文為衣婦人青帕籠髮如鍋圈

狀短衣長裙病不服藥用麵做虎

頭飾以綵線置簸箕內延鬼師禱

之性嗜酒惰於農

28. Guoquan (Pot-Ring) Gelao[48]

Adornment distinct from both the Miao and Gelao,
The Guoquan prefer twill, which they busily weave.
Wrapped in colorful threads, a molded tiger head
Is brought forth in a basket for Buddhist worship.

The Pot-Ring[48] Gelao are located in Pingyuan District. Men weave plant fibers into twill for tunics. Married women use dark kerchiefs to cover their hair in the shape of a pot ring. They wear short tunics and long skirts. When sick they do not take medicine. Rather, they make a tiger head using flour, decorate it with colorful thread, place it in a winnowing basket, and engage a shaman to pray. By nature they are fond of spirits and indolent when it comes to agriculture.

---

48. A "pot-ring" is an iron ring used to make the hole over a cooking stove smaller.

披袍仡佬 二十九

冶鐵爐邊種又分鑄犁為業最殷
勤婦人無事披袍坐細染羊毛織
彩裙

披袍仡佬在平遠州男子多鑄
犁為業婦人以青綫扎縛髮衣長
尺許外披以袍前長後短無領袖
洞其中以首貫之織五色羊毛為
綵裙性淳慎勤耕織

58　A Miao Album of Guizhou Province

29. Pipao (Cape) Gelao

By the metal-smelting furnace, yet one more kind.
Casting ploughshares by trade, they are most hard-working.
When women are not busy, wrapped in capes they sit
Weaving colorful skirts from carefully dyed wool.

Pipao Gelao are located in Pingyuan District. Men cast ploughshares by trade. Married women fasten a piece of dark cloth more than one foot long over their hair. They wrap themselves with outer capes that are long in front and short in back. The capes have no collars or sleeves, but have a hole through which to put the head. The Pipao Gelao weave sheep's wool of five different hues into colorful skirts. By nature honest and careful, they work diligently at weaving and tilling.

木狫三十

出郊祀鬼各紛然挽髻衡梳特地

偏新束草龍齊拜祝花衣相映

彩旗鮮

木狫所在多有王黎金文等

姓男子首裹青巾女子偏髻插

梳花衣短裙親死有喪服無哀

經長子守喪二十九日不出期滿

延巫祝荐名曰放鬼凡祀鬼束一

草龍上插五色紙旗往郊外祀

之時節則歌舞為歡冬令掘地

為爐卧牛羊皮而無被

30. Mulao

Pell-mell they enter the wild to pray to the ghosts.
Their knotted hair, fastened with combs, slants to one side.
Anew they form grass dragons; all alike worship.
Colorful clothing reflects light, bright flags glisten.

Mulao are found in many different localities. Their surnames include
Wang, Li, Jin, and Wen. Men wrap their heads with dark kerchiefs.
Women wear their hair up to one side with a comb inserted, and dress
in colorful tunics and short skirts. When a relative dies, the Mulao wear
mourning clothes but not coarse white hemp. The eldest son watches
over the corpse for twenty-nine days and does not go out. When the
period of mourning has been completed they engage a sorcerer to pray.
This is called releasing the ghost. Whenever sacrifices are made to
ghosts, they fashion a dragon from grass and insert five colored flags
into its back. They go out into the wild to sacrifice to it. Thereupon
they sing and dance for joy. In wintertime they dig a hole to make a
stove, and lay down on cow and sheep skins.[49] They do not have quilts.

---

49. *Niu* may refer more broadly here to water buffalo or oxen, not just cows.

犲獞三十一

内勤紡織外勤耕男女衣裙短
布成初祭親喪歌且舞直於臨
穴動哀情
犲獞在荔波縣男子善耕婦
女工織短衣短裙僅足蔽膝親
死不置棺以木板殮而停之互
相歌唱至葵子女哭必出血守
墳三日而返

62　*A Miao Album of Guizhou Province*

31. Ge Zhuang

Inside they spin and weave, outside they work the land.
Men and women's clothes are made from short lengths of cloth.
A parent lost, at the wake they still sing and dance.
Only at the burial are they moved to grief.

The Ge Zhuang are located in Libo County. Men are good at farming and women work at weaving.[50] They wear short tunics and short skirts that just barely cover the knee. When a parent dies, the Ge Zhuang do not lay the body out in a coffin, but rather dress it for burial and rest it on a plank. They then sing antiphonally until the actual burial. Sons and daughters cry their eyes out[51] and watch over the grave for three days before returning [home].

---

50. "Men till and women weave" is an ancient phrase that points to gendered productive roles for male and female subjects of the empire. Taxes were paid in grain and cloth until the mid-sixteenth century. As mentioned in the Introduction, *Illustrations of Tilling and Weaving* (Gengzhi tu) were imperially commissioned during the Song and Qing dynasties.

51. Literally, "till blood comes forth"—a saying that alludes to heavy crying.

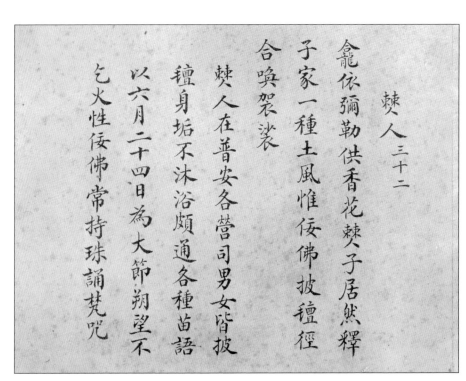

僰人三十二

龕依彌勒供香花僰子居然釋
子家一種土風惟倭佛披氈徑
合喚袈裟

僰人在普安各營司男女皆披
氈身垢不沐浴頗通各種苗語
以六月二十四日為大節朔望不
乞火性佞佛常持珠誦梵咒

64 *A Miao Album of Guizhou Province*

32. Boren

Incense, flowers, placed on Maitreya Buddha's shrine.
Devoting their lives to Buddha, some become priests.
One local custom is total faith in Buddha.
Buddhist monks' robes made from pieces of straight felt, joined.

Boren are located in every nook and cranny of Pu'an.[52] Both men and women wrap themselves in felt throws. Their bodies are dirty; they do not bathe. They are conversant in all of the Miao languages. The twenty-fourth day of the sixth month is their big festival. On the first and fifteenth of each month they do not light fires to make offerings.[53] Their nature is to put their faith in the Buddha. They often hold beads and recite Buddhist prayers and charms.

---

52. Literally, "every encampment and sub-district of Pu'an."

53. Because this is a common Buddhist practice, its absence is noted. It is not unusual in Taiwan today to see lit braziers for offerings to the spirits on the first and fifteenth day of the lunar cycle.

土人 三十三

元日迎魃便大儺連村擊鼓唱神
歌土人漸被華風染近日衣冠更
若何

土人所在多有在貴筑貴定廣
順者與軍民通婚姻歲時禮節
頗有華風婦人力耕作種植時
田歌相答清越可聽歲首迎山魈
逐村屯以為儺擊鼓唱神歌所
至之家皆酒食之

66 *A Miao Album of Guizhou Province*

33. Turen (Local People)

On New Year's Day sprites are welcomed, then exorcized.
Village after village beats drums, sings soulfully.
Gradually Turen are colored by Chinese styles—
Recently its been clothing and caps, what's next then?

Turen are found in many different localities. Those in Guizhu, Guiding, and Guangshun intermarry with both soldiers and commoners.[54] Their seasonal festivities have quite a Chinese flavor. Women have strength to cultivate the soil. At planting time, they sing field songs antiphonally. Clear and shrill, the sound is pleasing to the ear. At New Year's they welcome mountain sprites into the villages in order to exorcize them. They beat drums and sing soulful songs. Whomever's house [the musicians] go to, they are given wine and food.

---

54. These "soldiers and commoners" would have been Chinese settlers (*min*), not members of ethnic minority groups.

蠻人三十四

隊隊花裙間綠蓑登山臨水各
張羅乘閒便是漁蒐獵網得禽
魚尤較多

蠻人在新添丹行二司男子披
草蓑婦人著青衣花布短裙
喪祭殺牛歌舞惰耕作喜漁
獵以十月朔為大節祀鬼性獷
悍出入必帶刀弩

68　*A Miao Album of Guizhou Province*

34. Manren (Barbarian People)

Colorful skirts, rank on rank, amidst straw rain capes;
Up in the mountains, down by the streams, each sets snares.
Availing themselves of leisure, they fish and hunt
Netting birds and fish. Which catch is more plentiful?

Manren are located in Xintian and Danxing Sub-Districts. Men wear straw rain capes. Married women wear dark tunics and short skirts made from colorful cloth.[55] For burial sacrifices they slaughter cattle, sing, and dance. They are lazy when it comes to cultivating the soil, but are good at fishing and hunting. The first day of the tenth month is their big festival at which they perform sacrifices to ghosts. By nature they are fierce and violent. They always carry knives and crossbows when they go out.

---

55. Some albums read "*hua bian qun*," or, "skirt bordered with a pattern," which would be more attuned with what the illustration portrays here.

峒人三十五

出入真成比目魚非鏢即弩手無
虛峒人耐冷由来慣衣襯蘆花暖
有餘
峒人皆在下游多以苗為姓性猜
忌出入夫婦必偶手不離鏢弩飲
食辟鹽醬最耐冷冬採蘆花以
禦寒

35. Dongren (Cave People)

Sincere, they come and go paired like flatfishes' eyes[56]
With hands never empty grasping spear or crossbow.
Accustomed to it, the Dongren can bear the cold.
Lined with willow catkins their clothes are more than warm.

The Dongren all live near the lower reaches of streams. Many use "Miao" as their surname. By nature they are suspicious and envious. Whenever they go out husband and wife go together, and always carry a spear or crossbow. They avoid salt in their diet. Most tolerant of cold winters, they gather willow catkins to withstand the cold.

---

56. Flatfish, such as flounder, have two eyes on the same side of their head, hence the image of being "paired like flatfishes' eyes."

猺人本自粵西来卜築依然傍
水隈採藥入山春色好一編榜簿
避人閒

猺人在貴定自粵西遷来居必傍
溪澗以樹皮接續引水至家懶於
出汲男子皆青布短衣耕作之暇
則入山採藥沿寨行醫歲時祀祭
瓠有書曰榜簿圓印篆文義不
可觧珍為秘藏風俗謹厚路不
拾遺

36. Yaoren

The Yaoren originally came from Guangxi.
Divining, they build near the water as of yore.
In the mountains they pluck herbs amidst spring color.
One special book they do not let people open.

The Yaoren are located in Guiding where they moved from Guangxi Province. They build their houses close to rivers or streams so that water pipes made of tree branches can bring water directly into their houses. They thus avoid the necessity of fetching water every day. The men all wear short dark cotton tunics. They go into the mountains to gather medicinal herbs when not working in the fields, and practice medicine near the village. On the eve of the New Year, the Yaoren offer sacrifices to Pan Hu.[57] They have a book, called a *banbu*, written in seal script. They do not understand its meaning, but it is prized as a secret heirloom. The customs of the Yaoren are respectful and sincere. If they find an object on the road they do not pocket it.

---

57. For a description of Pan Hu, see note 45.

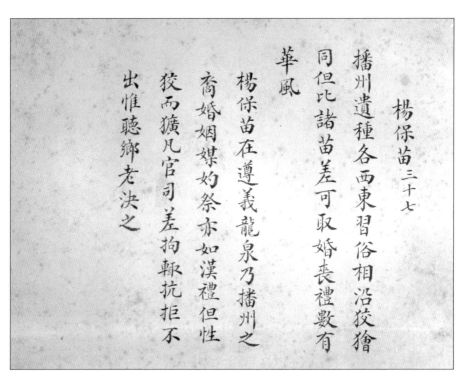

楊保苗三十七

播州遺種各西東習俗相沿狡獪
同但比諸苗差可取婚喪禮數有
華風

楊保苗在遵義龍泉乃播州之
裔婚姻媒妁祭亦如漢禮但性
狡而獷凡官司差拘輒抗拒不
出惟聽鄉老決之

37. Yangbao Miao

Bo Zhou's progeny are everywhere, east and west.
Their habits are at once cunning and compliant.
But compared with all Miao, they can be set apart;
Marriage and funeral rituals show Our influence.[58]

The Yangbao Miao are located in Zunyi and Longquan. They are the descendants of Bo Zhou.[59] In marriage the Yangbao Miao use a matchmaker, and their sacrifices are also like Han rituals. However, by nature they are crafty and fierce. Whenever an officer is sent to make an arrest they resist unceremoniously and will not go. They will only comply with what the village elder decides.

---

58. "Our influence" refers to that of the dominant Chinese culture.

59. Bo Zhou was a minority hereditary headman during the Yuan dynasty (1280 to 1368 C.E.). Bozhou is also the name of a district. Bo District was renamed Zunyi in 1728 when it was incorporated administratively into Guizhou from Sichuan.

狉猱苗三十八

忽然獵戶忽漁翁家在深山�
箐中喚作狉猱人莫辨祗緣服
飾異蠻風

狉猱苗即楊荒播之遺民也有
楊龍張石歐等姓在都勻石阡
黎平等處男子計口而耕女子
度身而織暇時以漁獵為事婚
喪相饋以犬所居門戶不扃出
入以泥封之服飾與漢人同

76　A Miao Album of Guizhou Province

38. Yanghuang Miao

Suddenly they're hunters, but then they're fishermen.
Homes nestled deep in the mountains in dense bamboo.
People cannot distinguish the Yanghuang if asked.
Only their clothing deviates from man[60] customs.

The Yanghuang Miao are the descendants of Yang Huang.[61] They have the surnames Yang, Long, Zhang, Shi, and Ou. They are located in Duyun, Shiqian, and Liping. The men farm according to their count of how many mouths there are to feed; the women weave according to their calculations of how many bodies there are to clothe. In their spare time the Yanghuang Miao fish and hunt. At weddings and funerals people present each other with dogs as gifts. They never lock the door when they go out, but seal it with mud. Their clothing is similar to that of the Han people.

---

60. *Man* is a general term that is usually translated as "southern barbarians."

61. Yang Huang was a hereditary chief during the Ming dynasty (1368–1644 C.E.). Although the characters are not the same, the name of the group may have derived from the name of this ancestor.

九股苗三十九

頭標白羽短青衣九股苗蠻勇
力稀手挽強弓身裹鐵口唧利
刀走如飛
九股苗在興隆衛凱里司武侯
南征後遺九人遂為九股衣尚
青頭標白羽性剽悍曳長弓曰
偏架三人共張矢無不貫有牛
尾鎗與九子炮相埒戴鐵盔披
短甲下用鐵練圍身鐵片裹腿
左手持木牌右手執標桿口唧
利刀捷走如飛

39. Jiugu (Nine-Divisions) Miao

With white feathers in their hair and short dark jackets,
The Jiugu Miaoman are courageous, strong, and few.
Powerful bows to hand, bodies wrapped in iron,
With sharp blades in their mouths, they walk as if they fly.

The Jiugu Miao are located in Xinglong and Kaili. After Zhuge Liang led his army on a southern expedition, nine persons remained there.[62] These nine became the ancestors of the Jiugu Miao. The Jiugu Miao like to wear dark clothes and they stick white feathers in their hair. By nature they are nimble and cruel. It is said that when they draw their long bows three men work together to string the arrow on the frame and that there is nothing it will not pierce. They also have "cattle-tail" spears and "nine-shot" cannons. They wear helmets on their heads, short armor on their upper bodies, iron chains around their waists, and iron sheets around their legs. In their left hands they carry wooden shields, in their right hands they hold spears, and in their mouths they hold sharp knives. They walk so fast they seem to fly.

---

62. Zhuge Liang's position is described in note 5.

八番苗四十

莫怪番苗一味慵　由来操作婦

能供家家薅稻連稭貯不到臨

炊不下舂

八番苗在定番州衣服同漢人

其俗男逸女勞婦女短髮作髻

日出而耕日入而織薅稻連稭儲

之剡木作臼曰椎塘必臨炊始取

稻把手舂之以十月望為大節親

死莫不擇期夜靜而出日不使

吾親知之

40. Bafan Miao

Do not blame the Fan Miao for being indolent;
Their womenfolk can manage the manual labor.
On reaping rice, each family stores it with the stalk.
Not until they want to eat do they husk the grain.

The Bafan Miao are located in Dingfan District. Their clothing is the same as that of the Han. Customarily the men are idle and the women work hard. The women have short hair which they dress. When the sun rises they work in the fields, when the sun sets they weave. Upon reaping rice they store it on the stalk. They hollow out wood to make a mortar called a *chui tang*, and only when they are ready to prepare it do they husk the rice by pounding it. Their most important festival is on the full moon of the tenth month. When a parent dies, they do not select a date for burial; instead they do it in the stillness of night. They say that this is so one's relatives will not know about it.

紫薑苗四十一

建子剛逢便換年紫薑風俗舊
相沿閉門七日渾無事榾柮頻
添晝穩眠

紫薑苗在都勻丹江平越清平
黃平等處以十一月朔為大節
閉門七日不出犯者以為不祥輕
生好鬥獲仇人輒生啖其肉夫
死必妻嫁而後葬曰喪有主矣

41. Zijiang (Purple-Ginger) Miao

Their New Year always begins with the jianzi month.[63]
The customs of the Zijiang are still as of old;
For seven days they close their doors and do nothing
Adding more firewood, they sleep soundly by day.

The Zijiang Miao are located in Duyun, Danjiang, Pingyue, Qingping, and Huangping. The first day of the eleventh month is their big festival. They close their doors for seven days and do not emerge. Those who break this rule are regarded as unlucky. The Zijiang Miao are belligerent and place little value on life. They eat the raw flesh of captured enemies. When the husband dies, the wife must remarry before the burial of her deceased husband. This is called "mourning has a leader."[64]

---

63. *Jianzi* refers to a month in the cyclical calendar. The *jianzi* month was set up as the start of the new year during the Zhou dynasty.

64. This phrase implies that the new husband would lead or host the funeral ceremonies.

谷蘭苗四二

青帕蒙頭織婦妝木棉初綻採
花忙布成入市人爭購土産如
斯俗最良

谷蘭苗在定番州性剽悍善
撃刺出入攜帶鏢弩諸苗畏
之男女皆短衣婦人髻蒙青
帕工紡織布極精客入市人爭
購之語曰欲作汙衫褲須得谷
蘭布婚姻亦用媒妁

42. Gulin Miao

Dressed as weaving women, heads decked with dark kerchiefs,
When kapok is downy, busily they harvest.
People vie to buy the finished cloth at market.
Local products like this are customs at their best.

The Gulin Miao are located in Dingfan. By nature they are nimble and cruel, and skilled at piercing with a sword. All Miao fear them. Both men and women wear short tunics. Women cover their heads with dark kerchiefs. They work at spinning and weaving. Their cloth is especially fine. When they go to market people compete to buy it. There is a saying, "If you want to make underwear, you must buy Gulin cloth." When the Gulin Miao marry they use a matchmaker.

克盍粘羊苗四十三

懸巖鑿穴愛高樓上下還須駕竹
梯陋俗閙尸全不覺至情賴有子
規啼

克盍粘羊苗在廣順州之金筑司
擇懸巖鑿穴而居駕竹梯上下
有高至百仞者耕不用犁戔鐯
發土覆而不芸親死不哭浩歌笑
舞謂之閙尸明年聞杜鵑聲則
舉家號泣曰鳥猶時至親不復
來矣

43. Kemeng Guyang Miao

In holes carved in tall cliffs, they love to roost up high.
To go up and down they need a bamboo ladder.
They fête the dead—vulgar custom—oblivious.
Only when they trust their feelings do children mourn.

The Kemeng Guyang Miao are located in Guangshun District's Jinzhu Sub-District. Selecting steep cliffs, they tunnel holes in them in which to dwell. They fashion bamboo ladders, some of which are as tall as 800 feet for going up and down. They engage in agriculture but use hoes and not ploughs to prepare the earth. They till, but do not weed. When a parent dies they do not cry, but sing, smile, and dance. This is called fêting the corpse. The next year when they hear the cry of the cuckoo, the whole family wails together. There is a saying that although birds come back at the same time every year, the dead are gone forever.

洞苗四十四

近水種棉多古風苗巾自織頗
精工花裙藍帕雖夷俗男子衣
衫與漢同
洞苗在天柱錦屏通漢語近
水而居以種棉花為葉男子
衣服與漢同故多為漢人傭
工女子戴藍布巾花邊織洞帕
頗工

88　A Miao Album of Guizhou Province

44. Dong (Cave) Miao

Raising cotton near water, most follow old ways.
They weave their own Miao kerchiefs, of fine workmanship.
'Though flowered skirts and blue kerchiefs are their custom,
Menfolk wear clothing that is the same as the Han.

The Dong Miao are located in Tianzhu and Jinping. They understand Chinese. They live close to water and cultivate cotton for a living. The men's clothing is like that of the Han Chinese, therefore many hire themselves out to work for the Han.[65] Women cover their heads with blue cloth kerchiefs edged with lace that requires a lot of labor to make.

---

65. While this may seem a *non sequitur*, the cause and effect ("therefore"), is clearly indicated in the original Chinese.

箐苗四十五

傍山居箐性多良喜種山禾亢勝

稻粱麻子採來供食饌麻皮織

去作衣裳

箐苗在平遠州居依山箐亦

青苗類也不善耕惟種山糧或

食麻子男女衣服均以麻皮自織

90　*A Miao Album of Guizhou Province*

45. Qian (Dense-Bamboo) Miao

On bamboo-clad slopes they dwell, by nature peaceful.
Skilled at growing mountain rice, good as paddy rice.
They collect the seeds of hemp, which they like to eat,
And weave their clothing from its outer coverings.

Living on mountainsides amid dense bamboo forests, the Qian Miao
are the same kind as the Qing Miao.[66] Not skilled at ploughing, they
only plant mountain grains. Some eat hemp seed. The clothing of men
and women alike is of hemp they weave themselves.

---

66. For Qing Miao, see figure 16.

狑家苗四十六

男女相歡自結婚直須生子始回
親仲冬祭鬼為年節藍帕蒙頭
一色新
狑家苗在荔波縣雍正十年自
廣西改隸於黎男女均藍花帕
蒙頭以十一月為歲首祭槃瓠
男女連袂相歌舞所悅者負之
而去及生子方歸母家名曰回
親始通媒過聘

92   *A Miao Album of Guizhou Province*

46. Lingjia Miao

Men and women, in love, bind themselves in marriage.
They must have a child before they return home.
At the mid-winter New Year's ghost sacrifices
Heads are covered with blue kerchiefs, all one shade—new.

Lingjia Miao are located in Libo County, which during the tenth year of the Yongzheng emperor's reign[67] changed from being under the jurisdiction of Guangxi to Guizhou. Both men and women cover their heads with blue kerchiefs. They consider the eleventh month to be the beginning of the year. They offer sacrifices to Pan Hu,[68] and men and women join sleeves and sing and dance together. If a man and woman fall in love, he carries her off on his back. Only after the birth of a child will they return to the mother's home. This is known as "going through a matchmaker and sending betrothal gifts only after returning home."

---

67. Equivalent to 1732.
68. For a description of Pan Hu, see note 45.

狪家苗四十七

勤儉由來說古狪䜌紀事不
嫺豐種棉自織衣仍短木刻傳
來有古風

狪家苗在荔波縣衣不過膝歲
首以魚肉祀䜌䜌極豐腆近水
而居善種棉女勤紡織男通漢
語而不識文字以木刻為信

47. Dongjia Miao

Diligent and thrifty, just like the ancient Dong,
They don't mind lavish sacrifices to Pan Hu.
They raise and weave cotton, yet their garments are short.
The ancient custom of notching wood is passed down.

The Dongjia Miao are located in Libo County. Their tunics do not extend below the knee. At the beginning of the year, they make excessively abundant sacrifices of fish and meat to Pan Hu.[69] They live close to water and are good at raising cotton. The women work hard at spinning and weaving. The men can speak Chinese, but are not familiar with written characters. They notch wood to make contracts.

---

69. For a description of Pan Hu, see note 45.

狄家苗四十八

重裙無袴漫相嘲綠線橫斜綴

袖梢青箬裹鹽摶糯飯掬泉細

嚼勝嘉肴

狄家苗在荔波縣男子四秋

長衣以裙為袴女子短衣窄

袖重裙無褲食惟糯飯無匕

箸以手摶之渴則飲水

48. Shuijia Miao

Layered skirts but no breeches, they mock each other,
The tips of their sleeves basted with colorful thread.
Salt and glutinous rice are wrapped in bamboo leaves.
They savor this with water as the best of fare.

The Shuijia Miao are located in Libo County. Men wear long tunics measuring over four feet, and skirts instead of pants. Women wear short tunics with narrow sleeves and layered skirts without breeches. For food they eat only glutinous rice. They do not use chopsticks, but seize it with their hands. When thirsty they drink water.

六額子四十九

六額子分黑白居丈夫尖髻女長
裙最憐尢後偏多憐折骨頻年洗
不虛

六額子在大定有黑白二種男尖
髻婦人長衣不著裙人死莫亦用
棺一年後延親戚以牲酒致祭發
塚取骨刷洗以白為度復裹而埋
之洗至七次乃止家人有病則云祖
先之骨不潔也再取洗之故又名
洗骨苗

49. Liu (Six) Ezi

The black and white Liu Ezi live separately.
Husbands wear pointy hairdos, women long garments.
Most pitiful, what's after death is inhuman;
Yearly the decaying bones are washed. It is true.

The Liu Ezi are located in Dading. There are two kinds, black and white. Men wear their hair up in a sharp point. Married women wear long tunics but not skirts. When someone dies they bury the body in a coffin. One year later they invite relatives and offer sacrifices of meat and wine to the deceased. As a matter of course they open the grave, take out the bones, and wash them until they are white. They then wrap them up and bury them again. The bone washing is carried out seven times, and then halted. If a family member should fall ill it is said that the bones of the ancestors are not clean, and therefore they wash them again. Because of this custom the Liu Ezi are also called Bone-Washing Miao.

長衣尖髻婦無裙死骨猶能臥故
墳底事相逢呼白額咆哮錯認是
此君山

白額子在貞豐羅斛等處男子
梳尖髻狀如螺蛳衣尚白婦女
長衣無裙其俗與六額子略同
惟疾病禱於鬼而不洗骨

白額子五十

50. Bai (White) Ezi

Long garments, pointed hairdos, women without skirts.
The bones of their dead are allowed to rest in graves.
"Why, when we meet up, do you call me Bai Ezi?"
He roars, "It is not so, I am a Liu Ezi!"[70]

The Bai Ezi are located in Zhenfeng and Luohu. Men comb their hair in a pointed spiral hairdo, and wear white. Married women wear a long tunic with no skirt. Their customs are similar to those of the Liu Ezi, but when someone becomes ill they pray to ghosts rather than washing the bones of the deceased.

---

70. The last two lines of this poem point to the difficulty in identifying the Liu Ezi and the Bai Ezi, possibly stemming from differences between Han and indigenous nomenclature. The issue may also reflect deeper questions of who has the power to define ethnic identity. *Ci jun* is interpreted as alluding to the previous entry.

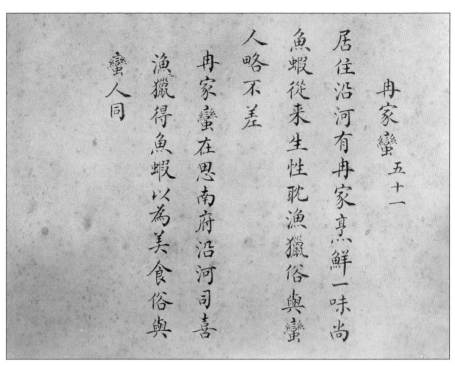

舟家蠻五十一

居住沿河有舟家烹鮮一味尚
魚蝦從來生性耽漁獵俗與蠻
人略不差
舟家蠻在思南府沿河司喜
漁獵得魚蝦以為美食俗與
蠻人同

51. Ranjia Man

The Ranjia all reside in Yanhe, "River's Edge."
When it comes to cooking they prefer fish and shrimp.
Their nature, from birth, is to love to hunt and fish.
Customs do not differ from those of the Manren.

The Ranjia Man are located in Sinan Prefecture's Yanhe Sub-District. They are good at fishing and hunting. When they catch fish or shrimp they treat it as a delicacy. Their customs are similar to those of the Manren.[71]

---

71. For the entry on Manren, see figure 34.

九名九姓苗五十二

九名九姓苗在獨山州性狡詐
多假揑姓名婚喪屠牛聚飲
醉必相鬥報以干戈擊之傷
人者納牛酒講和婦女以種
山為務俗與紫薑苗同

狡詐無端易姓名偶因小忿遂捐
生傷人不必投官狀攛酒牽牛
氣自平

104　A Miao Album of Guizhou Province

52. Jiuming Jiuxing (Nine-Names and Nine-Surnames) Miao

Deceitful and lacking principle, they change names.
Over a small matter they sometimes give their lives.
Perpetrators don't go before the magistrate;
Using wine and cattle they make peace by themselves.

The Jiuming Jiuxing Miao are located in Dushan District. Crafty and deceptive by nature, they often use false given names and false surnames. To celebrate weddings and funerals they slaughter cattle and come together to get drunk. There always has to be a fight; abruptly weapons appear and someone is struck. Those who cause injury offer cattle and wine as a way to settle the dispute. Women cultivate the mountainsides. Their customs are like those of the Zijiang Miao.[72]

---

72. For the entry on Zijiang Miao, see figure 41.

銀絲冠子綰長簪耳墜雙環項

數圈姑女別婚須賂舅子孫猶納

外甥錢

爺頭苗在古州性喜鬥耕不用

牛以人為之婦人編髮為髻戴

銀絲扇樣冠子綰以長簪耳墜

雙環項圈數圈短衣五色鑲之

姑之女必適舅之子舅無子姑

女必重賂其舅方許適人曰外甥

錢或不能措取償扵子孫

53. Yetou (Elderly-Headman) Miao

Caps made with silver thread, fastened by long hair pins,
Hoops dangle from their ears, large rings adorn their necks.
Upon marriage the bride must pay off her uncle;
His descendants will receive his niece's money.

The Yetou Miao are located in Guzhou. By nature they are bellicose. They use men rather than cattle to plow the fields. Married women coil their hair up and wear silver-colored fan-like hats attached with a long hair pin. They also wear a pair of earrings, several neck-rings, and short tunics bordered with five colors. A woman must marry the son of her mother's brother. If her maternal uncle has no sons, she must present the uncle with a monetary gift before she can marry anyone else. This is called money for the maternal uncle. The uncle, however, cannot spend the money received from his niece but must give it to his descendants.

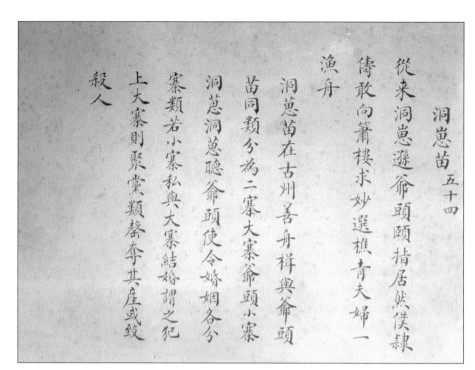

洞崽苗　五十四

從來洞崽遜爺頭頤措居然僕隸

儔敢向蕭樓求妙選樵青夫婦一

漁舟

洞崽苗在古州善舟楫與爺頭

苗同類分為二寨大寨爺頭小寨

洞崽洞崽聽爺頭使令婚姻各分

寨類若小寨私與大寨結婚謂之犯

上大寨則聚黨類螯奪其產或致

殺人

54. Dongzai Miao

The Dongzai have always yielded to the Yetou,
Whose arrogance presumes upon their servanthood.
If a Dongzai should dare to woo a Yetou girl,
The poor couple will only have a fishing boat.

The Dongzai Miao are located in Guzhou. They are good at boating and are the same kind as the Yetou Miao. The Dongzai Miao and Yetou Miao are divided into two stockades. The greater stockade contains the Yetou, and the lesser stockade the Dongzai. The Dongzai traditionally take orders from the Yetou Miao, and there is no intermarriage between the two groups. If someone from the lesser village should have illicit relations with someone from the greater village, this is regarded as a transgression against Yetou superiority. They will assemble and loot the property of the Dongzai transgressor, or even kill that person.

多將錦繡護胷前五色勻鑲女
袖邊若使牽牛賒聘禮百年猶
索鬼頭錢

八寨苗即黑苗也女子以五色布
鑲衣袖胸前錦繡一方護之各
寨均造一房曰馬郎房聽未婚男
女相聚其中訂婚以牛酒致聘嫁
三日即歸母家向婿索錢曰頭錢
弗與或別嫁有婚女皆死猶向其
子索之者謂之鬼頭錢

55. Bazhai (Eight-Villages) Miao

Many use embroidery to cover their chests.
Five colors also decorate the women's cuffs.
If a betrothal gift of cattle is delayed,
One hundred years later, "ghost money" is still owed.

Bazhai Miao are the same as Hei Miao.[73] Women use five-colored cloth to border the cuffs of their sleeves, and they wear a square of fine embroidery to cover their chests. Each village erects a house called the "groom's house" to allow unmarried men and women to come together. They arrange marriages among themselves using wine and cattle as betrothal gifts. Three days after the wedding they return to their parents' homes. The son-in-law is asked for money called "head money." If the son-in-law cannot pay, even if the bride marries someone else, or dies, her family can still ask the man to pay on behalf of her children. This is called "ghost head money."

---

73. For the entry on Hei Miao, see figure 17.

生性由来愛錦袍大環墜耳亦
堪豪婚姻何用通媒妁牛角杯
中飲濁醪

清江黑苗男女皆跣足廣種樹
木與漢人通商稱曰同年好著
錦袍寬襠褲以紅布束髮項
帶銀圈耳墜大環未婚男子
號曰羅漢女子號曰老陪春日
搆酒食於高岡男唱女和相悅
者飲以牛角遂成偶男子生子
乃曰有後方事耕作

56. Qingjiang (Clear-River) Hei (Black) Miao

Their nature, from birth, is to like fine brocade robes.
Large rings hang from their ears, also extravagant.
When marrying what's the use of a matchmaker?
Together they drink unstrained wine from a horn cup.[74]

Among the Qingjiang Hei Miao, both men and women go barefoot. They plant trees widely, and do business with the Han Chinese. This is called *tong nian*, being "of the same age." They like to dress in elegant robes and wide-bottomed trousers. They use a red cloth to bind their hair, wear silver hoops around the napes of their necks, and dangle large rings from their ears. Unmarried men are called "Luohan,"[75] and women are called "Laopei."[76] In the spring, they carry wine and food into the hills where the men sing and the women accompany them. If a man and woman like each other, they will drink together from an ox-horn cup, thus becoming a couple. When a man has a son, this is spoken of as having descendants to undertake agricultural work.

---

74. Technically, an ox- or cattle-horn cup.
75. The 500 disciples of Buddha were called Luohan.
76. "*Laopei*" translates literally as "venerable companion."

户户樓分上下林上樓八口下牛

羊男耕女織多安業不祀神祠

祀鬼堂

樓居黑苗在八寨丹江等處

男子耕種性剛而慈婦女以

羊角為髻好樓居牲畜即蓁

於樓下人死殮而停之以二十年

為期合寨共卜吉以百棺同葬公

建祖祠名曰鬼堂最信鬼其

地什物終毫不敢犯

114　*A Miao Album of Guizhou Province*

57. Louju (Storied-House-Dwelling) Hei (Black) Miao

Houses are split into upper and lower floors:
Family members above, animals down below.
Men till and women weave,[77] largely peaceful callings.
They sacrifice at the ghost hall, not to the gods.

The Louju Hei Miao are located in Bazhai and Danjiang. Men till and cultivate. They are unyielding and foolish by nature. Married women use sheep horn to dress their hair. They like to live in two-storey houses and raise animals in the lower storey. When someone dies, they dress the corpse for burial but then delay for up to twenty years. The whole village selects an auspicious date on which to bury a great number of coffins.[78] They collectively build an ancestral temple called the "ghost hall." They truly believe in ghosts and dare not make the tiniest infraction on the temple's land.

---

77. See note 50.
78. The texts says "one hundred coffins" but this is a symbolic rather than an exact figure.

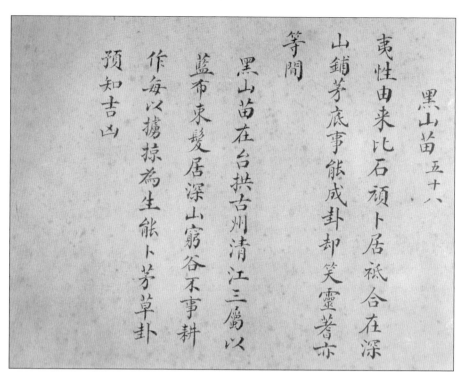

黑山苗五十八

夷性由来比石頑卜居祇合在深
山鋪芳底事能成卦却笑靈蓍亦
等間

黑山苗在台拱古州清江三屬以
藍布束髮居深山窮谷不事耕
作每以攄掠為生能卜芳草卦
預知吉凶

58. Hei Shan (Black Mountain) Miao

Barbarian by nature, obstinate as rock,
They choose to live enclosed in the deepest mountains.
Based on an arrangement of reeds, they can divine.
Yet they mock the use of milfoil divination.

The Hei Shan Miao are located in Taigong, Guzhou, and Qingjiang. They use blue cloth to bind their hair. They live deep in the mountains and in impoverished valleys. They do not engage in agriculture but live by capturing and plundering. They are able to foretell good and ill fortune by divining with reeds.

黑狆家五十九

慣栽檏木事生涯買得山林可

作家只為漢兒多要信殘骸殃

及保人家

黑狆家在清江廳以種檏為業

寨多富戶漢人往來其間可混

鄰里作保合夥生理借貸經商

無不應付倘折閱不妨直告尚可

再借或被詐騙則訪原保祖墳

摳取尸骸使之代追借項来贖

59. Hei (Black) Zhongjia

Accustomed to raising trees for a livelihood,
They buy wooded mountain land where they can build homes.
Only because many Han fail to meet their debts
Are the bones of the guarantor's ancestors harmed.

The Hei Zhongjia are located in Qingjiang Sub-District. They plant trees for a living. There are many wealthy households in the stockade, and they have interactions with the Han Chinese. They can ask their neighbors to serve as guarantors, forming a partnership. Whether regarding trade, lending money, or transacting business there is no request they will not honor. If the surety is lost, it does not matter; as long as the truth is told directly, they are allowed to borrow money again. However, if cheated, the lender will go to the graves of the original guarantor's ancestors, dig up the bones, and force the guarantor to pay back the money immediately.

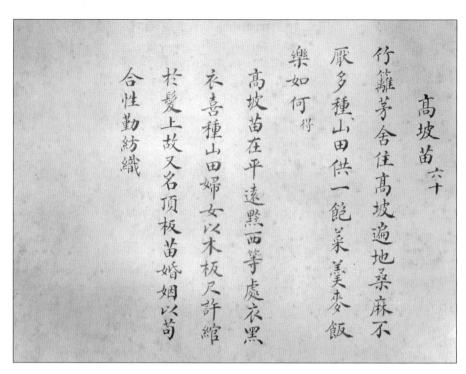

高坡苗六十

竹籬茅舍住高坡遍地桑麻不
厭多種山田供一飽菜羹麥飯
樂如何得

高坡苗在平遠黔西等處衣黑
衣喜種山田婦女以木板尺許綰
於髮上故又名頂板苗婚姻以苟
合性勤紡織

60. Gaopo (High Hill) Miao

Bamboo fences, thatched cottages, up in high hills
Mulberries and hemp everywhere. There is plenty.
Mountain fields contribute to their satiety.
Vegetables, soup, wheat, rice, is this not happiness?

The Gaopo Miao are located in Pingyuan and Qianxi. They wear black tunics and like to cultivate mountain fields. Women use small wooden boards, about one foot long, around which they coil their hair. Because of this custom they are also called Dingban (Board-Head) Miao. Marriage is determined by with whom they have shared illicit intercourse. By nature they are diligent at spinning and weaving.

平伐苗 六十一

草衣髳髴是爺家擕弩持鎗
俗又差喪祭婚姻都用犬入村
底怪吠聲譁

平伐苗在貴定之平伐司男子
草衣短裙善擊刺出入必持鎗
弩婦人短衣桶裙以長簪綰髮
人死以木槽瘞之婚喪皆用犬

61. Pingfa Miao

Grass garments, disheveled like an old grandpa's hair.
Carrying crossbows and spears, their customs are coarse.
Mourning sacrifices and weddings both use dogs.
In the village, what's strange? The sound of barking dogs.

The Pingfa Miao are located in Guiding County's Pingfa Sub-District. Men wear straw tunics and short skirts. They are skilled with swords. Coming and going they always carry a crossbow and spear. Married women wear short tunics and bucket skirts, and coil their hair up using a long hair pin. When someone dies, the Pingfa Miao bury the body in a wooden trough. Dogs are used at both weddings and funerals.[79]

---

79. The dogs would presumably be used for sacrifices or feasting (perhaps both), although the text does not state this explicitly. Note that the illustration shows a white dog being eviscerated.

黑生苗六十二

長鏢短劍鎮相隨富室從來少

了遺辜際

熙朝教雅化投戈頓使性情移

黑生苗在清江廳性凶悍訪富戶

所居輙明火執仗糾黨刦之自雍

正年間征服亦知守法

62. Hei (Black) Sheng (Wild or Raw) Miao

Always accompanied by long spears and short daggers—
Wealthy households have long since disappeared from here.
Happily refined during our glorious rule
They've surrendered their spears and their nature has changed.

The Hei Sheng Miao are located in Qingjiang Sub-Prefecture. By nature they are cruel. They would search out the homes of the wealthy and all at once, by torch light, seize weapons and band together to plunder them. However, during the reign of the Yongzheng emperor[80] they were reduced to submission, and now observe the law.

---

80. The Yongzheng emperor reigned from 1723 to 1735.

清江狪家六十三

耕作從來是婦人男兒驕悍性
難馴平時哨聚欺孤客索得腰
纏好贖身

清家狪家台拱亦有之婦人
勤耕織男子著紅巾腰佩大刀
每聚黨挐行路孤客長木為
枷枷之索取財物名曰贖身錢
弗與終不能脫近蒙嚴懲不
敢肆矣

63. Qingjiang (Clear-River) Zhongjia

Tending the fields has always been for the women.
The men are proud and cruel; by nature hard to tame.
They commonly waylay ordinary travelers
Demanding valuables to buy back their freedom.

Qingjiang Zhongjia[81] are also found in Taigong. The women are diligent at both weaving and working in the fields. Men, wearing red cloth on their heads, with large knives at their belts, band together to waylay solitary travelers. They collar them in a wooden yoke made from a tall tree and extort valuables from them called "redeem oneself money." If travelers do not pay, they will never be freed. Recently the Qingjiang Zhongjia were severely punished and so they dare not do this anymore.

---

81. This line actually begins "Qingjia Zhongjia," but this is undoubtedly a copyist's error. It should read Qingjiang Zhongjia (as in the heading).

里民子六十四

男兒貿易作生涯慶吊相通做
漢家婦女芒鞋全不襪纏完紡
績又桑麻
里民子在貴陽大定黔西清鎮
等處男子貿易為生婦女穿細
耳草鞋勤於耕作暇則織羊毛
布為衣好養牲畜常帶入山
歲時禮節與漢人同

64. Liminzi

All the men engage in trade for a livelihood.
Their ceremonies resemble those of the Han.
Women wear straw sandals without any stockings.
The spinning done, there are still mulberries and hemp.

Liminzi are located in Guiyang, Dading, Qianxi, and Qingzhen. Men engage in trade for a living. Women wear *xi er*[82] straw shoes and are diligent at agricultural work. In their spare time they weave wool into cloth for clothes. They like to raise animals and often lead them into the mountains. Their New Year's rites and festivals are similar to those of the Han.

---

82. *Xi er* translates literally as "fine-eared." It may, however, be a transliteration rather than a descriptive phrase.

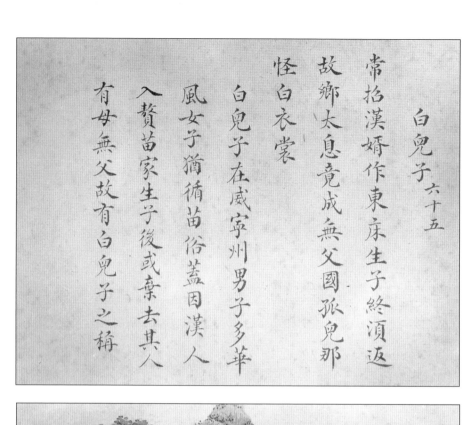

白兒子六十五

常招漢婿作東床生子終須返

故鄉太息竟成無父國孤兒那

怪白衣裳

白兒子在威寧州男子多華

風女子猶循苗俗蓋因漢人

入贅苗家生子後或棄去其人

有母無父故有白兒子之稱

65. Bai Erzi (White Sons)

The Bai Erzi welcome Han men as sons-in-law.
But, after fathering children they return home.
Alas! What an end! A nation without fathers.
Children without fathers; no wonder they wear white.

The Bai Erzi are located in Weining District. Men generally are acculturated, but the women retain the customs of the Miao. Han men enter the homes of Bai Erzi women as bridegrooms, but after the birth of a child, they often leave. The children, therefore, have mothers but no fathers; from this practice they get the name "fatherless sons."[83]

83. Although Bai Erzi means literally "white son," the meaning here is "fatherless son." The connection is not entirely clear. As suggested by the poem, it may stem from the Han association between white clothing and mourning (for a lost father).

白龍家六十六

龍家生性亦何奇市物從來不
手攜底事衣衫常著白婚喪
略倣漢威儀
白龍家在大定平遠等處衣
白衣入山採藥割漆以售於
市凡物皆背負之婚喪頗循
漢禮

66. Bai (White) Longjia

Why is the Longjia temperament so strange from birth?
They don't carry the goods they market with their hands.
Why is it that they customarily wear white,
Yet in weddings and funerals imitate the Han?

The Bai Longjia are located in Dading and Pingyuan. They wear white clothing, and go into the mountains to gather medicinal herbs and cut lacquer trees to sell at the market. All of these things they carry on their backs. In their weddings and funerals they follow Han rites.

白狃家 六十七

錦裙繡屨鬥門紅妝打要春來抵

月場到底外郎情不密斷郎還

要配新郎

白狃家在荔波縣男子頭戴狐尾

女子身小而甚淡藍色衣細褶匈

雲裙紅繡花鞋每春擇平壤剣

大木一節曰巴槽男女截竹擊之

謂之打要抱腰相戲父母觀而不

禁漢人通其語者亦可與私曰外

郎女有正配酬以布數端曰斷郎

禮遂絕往來

67. Bai (White) Zhongjia

All decked out[84] in brocade skirts and embroidered shoes,
Drumming to make spring come, they reach the moonlit grounds.
The affections of outside lovers are not sure;
She breaks up, and returns to pair with a bridegroom.

The Bai Zhongjia are located in Libo County. Men wear fox tails on their heads. Women are slight of stature and quick-witted. They wear light-blue tunics, finely-pleated "enticing cloud" skirts,[85] and shoes embroidered with red thread. Every spring they select a flat area, cut down a section of a large tree, and celebrate a festival called *ba cao*. Men and women cut bamboo sticks to drum on it. This is called drumming to prompt embracing. They sport together and their parents look on and do not prohibit it. Han who can understand the Bai Zhongjia language can also have private relations with them. These are called gentlemen from outside. If a girl then forms a proper match with someone else, she will give the former lover several lengths of cloth, called a "breaking up" gift. They then break off their relationship.

---

84. The Chinese conveys a sense of competition among unmarried women for the nicest appearance, which is not conveyed directly in the translation.

85. *Gou yun* is the Chinese name rendered as "enticing cloud."

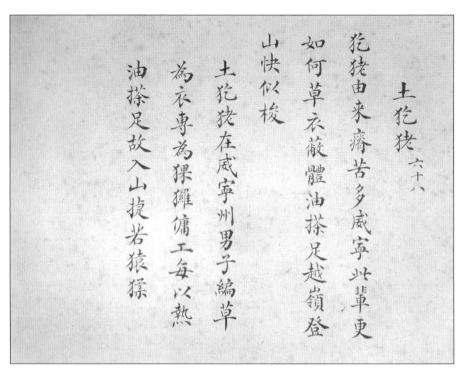

土犵狫 六十八

犵狫由來瘠苦多威寧此輩更
如何草衣蔽體油搽足越嶺登
山快似梭

土犵狫在威寧州男子編草
為衣專為猓玀傭工每以熱
油搽足故入山捷若猿猱

68. Tu (Local) Gelao

The Gelao have always had a hard time of it.
But those who live in Weining have it even worse.
Straw cloaks shade their bodies, oil covers their feet.
They move through mountains fast as a weaver's shuttle.

The Tu Gelao are located in Weining District. Men weave straw into tunics and hire their labor out to the Luoluo.[86] They all rub their feet with hot oil. For this reason they can enter the mountains swift as monkeys.

---

86. For the entry on Luoluo, see figure 1.

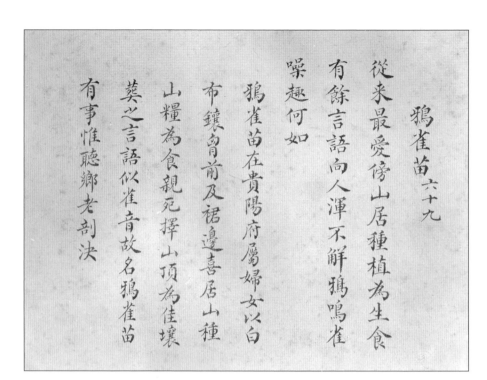

鴉雀苗六十九

從來最愛傍山居種植為生食
有餘言語向人渾不解鴉鳴雀
噪趣何如
鴉雀苗在貴陽府屬婦女以白
布鑲胷前及裙邊喜居山種
山糧為食親死擇山頂為佳壤
葵之言語似雀音故名鴉雀苗
有事惟聽鄉老剖決

69. Yaque (Crow and Sparrow) Miao

They have always loved living in the mountains best.
Farming for a living, food is more than ample.
Completely unintelligible, their speech is
Amusing, like cawing crows and chirping sparrows. birds

The Yaque Miao are located under the jurisdiction of Guiyang Prefecture. Women use white cloth to make borders around the front of their bodices and the hems of their skirts. They like to live in the mountains and grow mountain grain for food. When a relative dies they select a mountain top as an auspicious place for burial. Their language resembles the sounds of small birds. For this reason they are called Crow and Sparrow Miao. Important matters must be decided only by village elders.

葫蘆苗七十

此輩由來賦性殊耕桑不事事
穿窬葫蘆大抵都依樣妙手
丹青畫不如
葫蘆苗在定番羅斛等處性
凶暴連群聚黨專以刼搶為
事不事耕織近來嚴懲亦知
守法

70. Hulu (Gourd) Miao

The natural talents of this kind distinguish them:
They don't till or tend mulberries, but burgle homes
By boring holes. All of the Hulu are like this.
Their finesse unmatched even by a skilled artist.

The Hulu Miao are located in Dingfan and Luohu. By nature they are fierce and cruel. They join together forming gangs in order to rob people. This is what they do; they do not work at tilling or weaving. Recently they were severely punished and now know to observe the law.

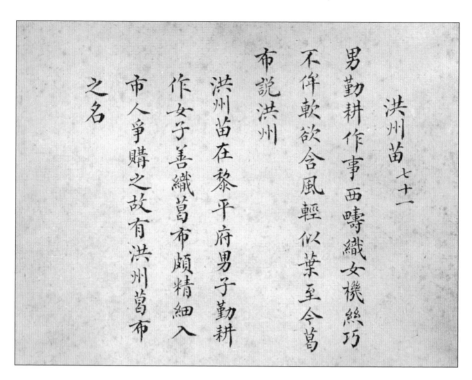

洪州苗七十一

男勤耕作事西疇織女機絲巧
不俟軟欲含風輕似葉至今葛
布說洪州
洪州苗在黎平府男子勤耕
作女子善織葛布頗精細入
市人爭購之故有洪州葛布
之名

71. Hongzhou Miao

Men diligently farm; their business is the land.
Women weavers loom silk; their skill is unequaled.[87]
Pliable, soft as the breeze, and weightless as leaves,
When ge cloth is mentioned, one speaks of the Hongzhou.

The Hongzhou Miao are located in Liping Prefecture. Men are diligent in farming. Women are good at weaving extremely fine *ge* cloth of exquisite quality.[88] In the market, people vie with each other to buy it. Therefore Hongzhou *ge* cloth is famous.

---

87. See note 50.
88. The *ge* is a creeping edible bean, the fibers of which are used to make cloth for summer wear.

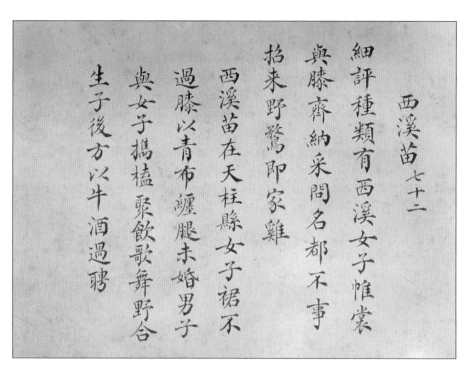

西溪苗七十二

細評種類有西溪女子帷裳

與膝齊納采問名都不事

招来野鶩即家雞

西溪苗在天柱縣女子裙不

過膝以青布纏腿未婚男子

與女子攜榼聚飲歌舞野合

生子後方以牛酒過聘

144　*A Miao Album of Guizhou Province*

72. Xiqi (West-Stream) Miao

A detailed discussion must include the Xiqi.
The clothing of the women reaches to the knee.
Bride-price is not paid, nor horoscopes consulted.
They call for a wild duck, yet get a tame chicken.[89]

The Xiqi Miao are located in Tianzhu County. The skirts of the women do not reach below the knee, and they wrap their legs with dark cloth. Unmarried men take food to the girls. They come together, drink, sing, dance, and have illicit intercourse. Only after a child is born are betrothal gifts of cattle and wine bestowed.

---

89. This phrase is probably an allusion to their courtship and marriage practices: although they engage in illicit liaisons which might not be expected to last (wild ducks fly off), their partners become part of the domestic scene (tame chickens).

73. Chezhai Miao[90]

The "Six-Hundred Wild Miao" are not of the same kind.
Although called Chezhai, they tend toward Chinese customs.
But they choose their own mates according to desire.
Boys and girls sing together in the wilderness.

Among the Chezhai Miao, men diligently sow and plant. Women labor at needlework. Those who are unmarried use a wilderness area as a place to dance under the moonlight. The men play stringed instruments and the women sing. The sound is pure and beautiful, unparalleled among all of the Miao. Those who find each other pleasing pair off on their own. This is also called "dancing under the moon." This kind of Miao were soldiers of Mao Sanbao.[91] Because six hundred of them married into the households of Miao women, they are called "Six Hundred Households Wild Miao."[92] They are located in Guzhou.

---

90. The text for this page was missing in the album reproduced here. This text is from an album in the collection of the Società Geografica Italiana (Chinese Catalog no. 60), in which it appears as the seventy-fifth entry.

91. Ma Sanbao is said to have taken refuge among the Miao when Wu Sangui, for whom he served as general, was defeated in the Revolt of the Three Feudatories during the reign of the Kangxi emperor. See Tapp and Cohn, *Tribal Peoples of Southwest China*, 70.

92. In Chinese, this is *Liubai hu zhi Sheng Miao*. This is undoubtedly the same as the "Six-Hundred Wild Miao" referred to more elliptically in the poem.

生苗七十四

火食民間自古同此鄉廢盡
遂皇功豚魚生噉稱佳味大
有茹毛飲血風
生苗在台拱凱里黃平施秉
等處多野性所食皆生物
魚肉以半熟為鮮故名生苗

74. Sheng (Wild or Raw) Miao

The people's provisions are just like as of old;
These villages reject imperial merit.
Suckling pig and fish, raw, have "excellent flavor."
Munching fur and quaffing blood are customary.[93]

The Sheng Miao are located in Taigong, Kaili, Huangping, and Shibing. They are generally wild by nature and eat any living thing. Since they believe that half-cooked fish and meat are the most delicious foods, they are called "raw" Miao.[94]

---

93. *Ru mao yin xue*, the expression translated here as "munching hair and quaffing blood" is a set phrase used to indicate savagery.

94. *Sheng* can mean either "wild" or "raw." The explanation here, that they are called "raw" Miao because they eat raw things is not standard, but it is an interesting example of etymological back-formation.

黑脚苗七十五

黑脚白翎暴客多挺身到處
逞干戈今朝有事疑難決試
向盆中鬥翠螺
黑脚苗在清江台拱等處男
子短衣大褲首插白翎出入三
五成羣持鏢帶刀以搶刦為能
凡事以螺螄二枚置盆中觀其
鬥以卜吉凶婦人夫死不再嫁
其男子不事刦奪者則無人
女嫁之

75. Hei Jiao (Black-Foot) Miao

"Black feet" and white feathers, most of them are brigands.
Chests out-thrust, they brandish their weapons everywhere.
If something comes up that's difficult to settle
They examine blue snails fighting in a basin.

The Hei Jiao Miao are located in Qingjiang and Taigong. The men wear short tunics and oversized pants. They stick white feathers in their hair. They come and go in bands of three to five, carrying spears and knives. They rob people for a living. When something important must be decided, they put two snails in a basin and watch them fight. From the result, they divine good or bad fortune. If a woman's husband dies, she does not remarry. No one is willing to give a daughter in marriage to a man who does not rob and fight.

黑樓苗七十六

共築虛堂似哨樓鼓聲震慶起
戈矛議團各寨遵鄉約執肯違
期失一牛

黑樓苗在清江八寨等處鄰近
諸寨共於平坦處建一樓名曰眾
堂懸大木一段刻其中凡有不平之
事登樓擊之如鼓音各寨相聞
帶鏢弩齊至樓下聽寨長指揮
有事之家備牛酒款之無故不
到者罰牛一頭以充公用

76. Hei Lou (Black Storied-House) Miao

They build an open structure like a watch tower.
At the sound of drumming, they raise their swords and spears.
The villages confer, then obey the headmen.
Those who don't show up are fined one head of cattle.

The Hei Lou Miao are located in Qingjiang and Bazhai. All of the closely neighboring villages together construct a storied building called an assembly hall on a piece of flat land. In it they hang up a large piece of wood that has been hollowed out inside. Whenever there is an injustice the victim will climb up the tower and beat on this piece of wood. When they hear the drumming the people from each village must assemble beneath the hall with their weapons and crossbows and listen to the commands of the village headmen. The person with the grievance prepares beef and wine to entertain those gathered to help him. If anyone does not show up without [having] a [good] reason, that person will be fined one head of cattle, which will be used collectively by the group.

短裙苗七十七

短裙著號信無差䕞草叢中

婦女詳露到腰臍先可詫那堪

下體不全遮

短裙苗在都匀八寨等處男

子短衣寬褲婦女短衣無領

袖從頭上籠下前不掩腹後

不遮腰其裙長五寸許細褶

而厚聊以蔽羞而已採䕞草

為業性嗜酒醉則卧山中隆

冬浴於溪澗云可助暖

77. Duanqun (Short-Skirt) Miao

The epithet "short skirt" is true; there's no mistake.
In the gromwell[95] thickets women raise a hubbub.
One first wonders at their exposed belly buttons,
But how can they bear to show their lower bodies?

The Duanqun Miao are located in Duyun and Bazhai. Men wear short tunics and baggy pants. Women also wear short tunics without collar or sleeves that slip on over the head and hang down, neither concealing the belly in front nor covering the waist in back. Their skirts are only a bit more than five *cun*[96] in length. They are finely pleated, full, and moreover barely cover their privates. The Duanqun Miao pick gromwell for a living. They are fond of hard drink. Once they are drunk, they just lie down in the mountains. They say that bathing in a stream in winter can warm a person up.

---

95. The Latin name for gromwell is *Lithospermum officinale*. The common Chinese name would translate literally as "purple grass." Gromwell is a plant that yields a purple dye.

96. A *cun* is a Chinese unit of length equal to one-third of a decimeter.

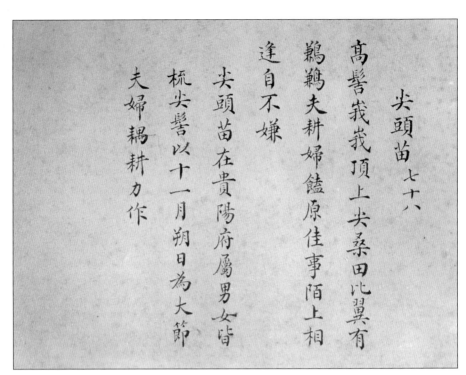

尖頭苗七十八

高髻峩峩頂上尖桑田比翼有
鶼鶼夫耕婦饁原佳事陌上相
逢自不嫌

尖頭苗在貴陽府屬男女皆
梳尖髻以十一月朔日為大節
夫婦耦耕力作

78. Jiantou (Pointed-Head) Miao[97]

Their lofty hair-styles are pointy at the top.
In the mulberry orchards couples are as one.[98]
The husband tills. The wife brings food. As it should be.
Whenever they meet on the path they do not mind.

The Jianding Miao are located under the jurisdiction of Guiyang Prefecture. Both men and women comb their hair up into a sharp point. Their big festival is on the first day of the eleventh month. Man and wife work together in the fields.

---

97. Jiantou Miao are sometimes called Jianding Miao.

98. This line contains several allusions to a mythical bird that, having only one wing, needed to pair up with a mate in order to fly. The image is a metaphor for husband and wife.

郎慈苗七十九

人情最謬是郎慈生子常須父
乳之男逸女勞沿舊俗漫從鴻案
效齊眉

郎慈苗在威寧州其俗男逸女
勞婦人產子必夫在房守之彌
月方出產婦則耕作以為養夫
除乳兒外無所事事父母將死
候氣絕拗其首轉向背曰好看
後人

79. Langci (Virtuous and Kind) Miao

The Langci display the oddest of sentiments.
When a child is born the father must care for it.
By old custom men are idle and women work.
As they are pacified, they act like man and wife.

The Langci Miao are located in Weining District. Their custom is for men to be at leisure and women to work. When a married woman gives birth to a child, her husband must stay at home for a month to care for it. After a full month he may go out. The woman who gave birth works in the fields to support them. The husband does nothing but nurse the child. When parents are dying, just at their last breath, their heads are broken off and twisted so that they face backwards. The Langci Miao believe that in this way their parents will be able to witness their descendants even after death.99

---

99. A more literal translation of this sentence would be, "This is known as having a good look at one's descendants."

羅漢苗 八十

男兒頭上一狐毛彌勒龕前禮
拜勞每至禁烟三月節佛天歡
喜奏琅璈
羅漢苗在八寨丹江等處男
子頭戴狐尾披髮於後最敬
彌勒佛每三月三日男女攜食
物歌舞供佛三日不食从肴寒
食之意

80. Luohan (Arhat) Miao

Men and boys, wearing fox fur on their heads, worship
Earnestly before Maitreya Buddha's shrine. At
The annual festival where smoke is forbidden,
The Buddhist heaven delights in the music made.

The Luohan Miao are located in Bazhai and Danjiang. Men wear fox tails on their heads and their hair down in back. They greatly revere Maitreya Buddha. On the third day of the third month, men and women bring food, and sing and dance, as offerings to Maitreya. They do not eat for three days; the meaning of this is similar to the Cold Food Festival.[100]

---

100. The Cold Food Festival (*hanshi*) is observed by the Han one day before Qing Ming, during which the Chinese pay their respect at the graves of their ancestors.

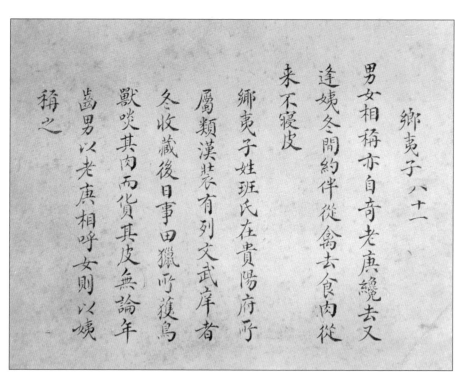

鄉夷子八十一

男女相稱亦自奇老庚繞去又
逢姨冬間約伴從禽去食肉從
來不寢皮

鄉夷子姓班氏在貴陽府所
屬類漢裝有列文武庠者
冬收藏後日事田獵叮獲鳥
獸啖其肉而貨其皮無論年
齒男以老庚相呼女則以姨
稱之

81. Xiang Yizi (Village Tribes)

Men and women mingle; it's odd to be alone.
The "old one" has just gone, now here is "auntie" too.
In winter, in parties, they follow birds and hunt.
They eat the meat, but do not use skins for sleeping.

The Xiang Yizi have the surnames Ban and Shi. They are under the jurisdiction of Guiyang Prefecture. Their manner of dress is similar to that of the Han, having distinctions between civil, military, and village scholar. In winter, after the harvest, they usually go hunting. They eat the meat of the birds and animals they capture, but sell the skins. No matter what their age, the men call each other "old one." Women are called "auntie."

82. Liudong (Six-Cave) Yiren[101]

The Liudong Yiren have extravagant customs.
They snip cloth, swap belts; no need for a matchmaker.
Literate, skilled at the loom, how marriageable!
They are the most powerful of the eighty-two.

The Liudong Yiren wear short tunics, colorful skirts, and flowery sleeves. Pointy boots are extended with cloth to the knee. Unmarried men and women trim pieces from their clothing [for each other] and exchange belts. They then divine [an auspicious day] and marry. Several tens of girls who live nearby hold a cloth umbrella over the bride, accompanying her and seeing her off. This is called *"song qing,"* accompanying a bride to her husband's house. Upon arriving at the man's home they are welcomed with singing and dancing. This goes on for three days and nights. Then the new bride is led back to her mother's house. Every night the groom sneaks in to sleep with her. Only after bearing a child does a woman move in with her in-laws. They are under the jurisdiction of Liping Prefecture.

---

101. The text for this page is missing from the album reproduced here. The translation has therefore been supplied from another album; see Ruey, *Fan Miao hua ce*, 4.

Bibliography

Alloula, Malek. *The Colonial Harem.* Minneapolis: University of Minnesota Press, 1986.

Asad, Talal, ed. *Anthropology and the Colonial Encounter.* London: Ithaca Press, 1973.

Birrell, Anne. *Chinese Mythology: An Introduction.* Baltimore: Johns Hopkins University Press, 1993.

"Bai Miao tu yong." Guizhou Nationalities Research Institute, 012508–012513 /K892.316/1988.II.22.

Blum, Susan D. *Portraits of "Primitives": Ordering Human Kinds in the Chinese Nation.* Lanham, Md.: Rowman and Littlefield, 2001.

Bremen, Jan van, and Akitoshi Shimizu, eds. *Anthropology and Colonialism in Asia and Oceania.* Richmond, Surrey: Curzon Press, 1999.

Brose, Michael. "Realism and Idealism in Yuan Dynasty Ethnography." Paper presented at Crossing the Borders of China: A Conference on Cross-cultural Interactions in Honor of Professor Victor H. Mair, University of Pennsylvania, Pa., December 5–7, 2003.

Bucher, Bernadette. *Icon and Conquest: A Structural Analysis of the Illustrations of de Bry's Great Voyages.* Chicago: University of Chicago Press, 1982.

Cheung, Siu-woo. *Appropriating Alterity: Miao Ethnicity and China's Politics of Recognition.* Seattle: University of Washington Press, forthcoming.

Chuang, Chi-fa. *Xie Sui "zhigong tu" manwen tushuo jiaozhu.* Taipei: Guoli Gugong Bowuyuan, 1989.

———. *"Xie Sui zhigong tu yanjiu"* (A Study of the Tribute-Presenting Scroll by Hsieh Sui). Proceedings of the 1991 Taipei Art History Conference, National Palace Museum, Taipei, 1992.

Clifford, James. *The Predicament of Culture: Twentieth-Century Ethnography, Literature, and Art.* Cambridge, Mass.: Harvard University Press, 1988.

Corrigan, Gina. *Miao Textiles From China.* Seattle: University of Washington Press; London: The British Museum, 2001.

Crossley, Pamela Kyle. *A Translucent Mirror: History and Identity in Qing Imperial Ideology.* Berkeley: University of California Press, 1999.

Daqing lichao shilu: Qing Gaozong chun huangdi shilu. (Veritable records of the Qing dynasty for the Qianlong emperor's reign). Taipei: Hualian chubanshe, 1964.

Diamond, Norma. "Defining the Miao: Ming, Qing, and Contemporary Views." In *Cultural Encounters on China's Ethnic Frontiers,* pp. 91–116. Ed. Stevan Harrell. Seattle: University of Washington Press, 1995.

Dikötter, Frank. *The Discourse of Race in Modern China.* London: C. Hurst, 1992.

Edkins, J. "The Miau Tsi Tribes: Their History." *The Chinese Recorder and Missionary Journal* 1 (July 1870): 30–36.

————. "The Miau Tsi." *The Chinese Recorder and Missionary Journal* 2 (August 1870): 74–76.

Elliott, Mark C. *The Manchu Way: The Eight Banners and Ethnic Identity in Late Imperial China.* Stanford: Stanford University Press, 2001.

Emperor Kangxi and Jiao Bingzhen. *Le Gengzhitu: Le livre du riz et de la soie.* Trans. Bernard Fuhrer. Paris: J. C. Lattès, 2003.

Gilman, Sander L. *Difference and Pathology: Stereotypes of Sexuality, Race, and Madness.* Ithaca: Cornell University Press, 1985.

————. "Introduction: What Are Stereotypes and Why Use Texts to Study Them?" In *Difference and Pathology: Stereotypes of Sexuality, Race, and Madness,* pp. 15–35. Ed. Sander L. Gilman. Ithaca: Cornell University Press, 1985.

Gladney, Dru C. "Representing Nationality in China: Refiguring Majority/Minority Identities." *Journal of Asian Studies* 53, no. 1 (February 1994): 92–123.

————. *Muslim Chinese: Ethnic Nationalism in the People's Republic.* Harvard East Asian Monographs, Vol.149. 2nd ed. Cambridge, Mass.: Council on East Asian Studies, Harvard University, 1996.

————. ed. *Making Majorities: Constituting the Nation in Japan, Korea, China, Malaysia, Fiji, Turkey, and the United States.* Stanford: Stanford University Press, 1998.

Guo Zizhang. *Qian ji* (A record of Guizhou province), 1608.

Hansen, Mette Halskov. *Lessons in Being Chinese: Minority Education and Ethnic Identity in Southwest China.* Seattle: University of Washington Press, 1999.

Harrell, Stevan. "Civilizing Projects and the Reaction to Them." In *Cultural Encounters on China's Ethnic Frontiers,* pp. 3–36. Ed. Stevan Harrell. Seattle: University of Washington Press, 1995.

————, ed. *Cultural Encounters on China's Ethnic Frontiers.* Seattle: University of Washington Press, 1995.

————. "The History of the History of the Yi." In *Cultural Encounters on China's Ethnic Frontiers,* pp. 63–91. Ed. Stevan Harrell. Seattle: University of Washington Press, 1995.

————, ed. *Perspectives on the Yi of Southwest China.* Berkeley: University of California Press, 2001.

————. *Ways of Being Ethnic in Southwest China.* Seattle: University of Washington Press, 2001.

Harrell, Stevan, Bamo Qubumo, and Ma Erzi. *Mountain Patterns: The Survival of Nuosu Culture in China.* Seattle: University of Washington Press, 2000.

Herman, John. "National Hegemony and Regional Hegemony: The Political and Cultural Dynamics of Qing State Expansion, 1650–1750." Ph.D. diss., University of Washington, 1993.

————. "Empire in the Southwest: Early Qing Reforms to the Native Chieftain System." *Journal of Asian Studies* 56, no.1 (1997): 47–74.

Hevia, James L. "Lamas, Emperors, and Rituals: Political Implications of Qing

Imperial Ceremonies." *Journal of the International Association of Buddhist Studies* 16, no. 2 (1993): 243–278.

Hodgen, Margaret. *Early Anthropology in the Sixteenth and Seventeenth Centuries.* Philadelphia: University of Pennsylvania Press, 1964.

Hostetler, Laura. "Chinese Ethnography in the Eighteenth Century: Miao Albums of Guizhou Province." Ph.D. diss., University of Pennsylvania, 1995.

———. *Qing Colonial Enterprise: Ethnography and Cartography in Early Modern China.* Chicago: University of Chicago Press, 2001.

———. "Qing Connections to the Early Modern World: Ethnography and Cartography in Eighteenth-Century China." *Modern Asian Studies* 34, no. 3 (2000): 623–62.

———. "Qing Views of Europeans in the *Huang Qing zhigong tu* (Qing imperial illustrations of tributary peoples)." Paper presented at The Age of Antiquaries in Europe and China Conference, Bard Graduate Center, New York, March 25–27, 2004.

Howell, David L. "The Ainu and the Early Modern Japanese State, 1600–1868." In *Ainu: Spirit of a Northern People,*" pp. 96–101. Ed. William W. Fitzhugh and Chisato O. Dubreuil. Washington, D.C.: Arctic Studies Center, National Museum of Natural History, Smithsonian Institution; Seattle: University of Washington Press, 1999.

Huang Qing zhigong tu (Qing imperial illustrations of tributary peoples). *Qinding Siku Quanshu* edition, 1761.

Hucker, Charles. *A Dictionary of Official Titles in Imperial China.* Stanford: Stanford University Press, 1985.

Jaeger, F. "Über Chinesische Miaotse-Albums." *Ostasiatische Zeitschrift* (Berlin). 5 (1917): 81–89.

Jenks, Robert D. *Insurgency and Social Disorder in Guizhou: The "Miao" Rebellion 1854–1873.* Honolulu: University of Hawaii Press, 1994.

Kakizaki Hakyo to sono jidai. Hokkaidoritsu Hakodate Bijutsukan, 1991.

Kaltenmark, Maxime. *Dictionnaire des mythologies.* Paris: Flammarion, 1981.

Kaup, Katherine Palmer. *Creating the Zhuang: Ethnic Politics in China.* Boulder: Lynne Rienner, 2000.

Kodama Sakuzaimon. *Ainu Historical and Anthropological Studies.* Sapporo: Hokkaido University School of Medicine, 1970.

Koshizaki Soichi. *Ainu eshi* (Illustrations of the Ainu). Sapporo: Maruzen Kabushiki Kaisha Sapporo Shiten Hatsubai, 1959.

Ledderose, Lothar. *Ten Thousand Things: Module and Mass Production in Chinese Art.* Princeton: Princeton University Press, 2000.

Lewis, Martin W., and Kären E. Wigen. *The Myth of Continents: A Critique of Meta-Geography.* Berkeley: University of California Press, 1997.

Li Zongfang. *Qian ji* (A record of Guizhou province), 1834.

Lin, Yueh-hwa. "The Miao-man Peoples of Kweichow." *Harvard Journal of Asiatic Studies* 5 (1940): 261–345.

Link, Perry. *Evening Chats in Beijing: Probing China's Predicament*. New York: Norton, 1992.

Litzinger, Ralph A. *Other Chinas: The Yao and the Politics of National Belonging*. Durham: Duke University Press, 2000.

Lombard-Salmon, Claudine. *Un exemple d'acculturation chinoise: la province du Guizhou au xviiiᵉ siècle*. Paris: École Française d'Extrême Orient, 1972.

MacRitchie, David. *The Aïnos*. Leiden: P.W.M. Trap, 1892.

Mair, Victor H. "The Book of Great Deeds: A Scripture of the Ne People." In *Religions of China in Practice*, pp. 405–422. Ed. Donald S. Lopez, Jr. Princeton: Princeton University Press, 1996.

McKhann, Charles. "The Naxi and the Nationalities Question." In *Cultural Encounters on China's Ethnic Frontiers*, pp. 39–62. Ed. Stevan Harrell. Seattle: University of Washington Press, 1995.

McNeill, William H. *The Rise of the West: A History of the Human Community*. Chicago: University of Chicago Press, 1963.

Michaud, Jean, and Christian Culas. "The Hmong of the Southeast Asia Massif: Their Recent History of Migration." In *Where China Meets Southeast Asia: Social and Cultural Change in the Border Regions*, pp. 98–121. Eds. Christopher Hutton, Grant Evans, and Kuah Khun Eng. New York: St. Martin's Press; Singapore: Institute of Southeast Asian Studies, 2000.

Mueggler, Erik. *The Age of Wild Ghosts: Memory, Violence, and Place in Southwest China*. Berkeley: University of California Press, 2001.

Oakes, Tim. *Tourism and Modernity in China*. New York: Routledge, 1998.

Ohnuki-Tierney, Emiko. "A Conceptual Model for the Historical Relationship Between the Self and the Internal and External Others: The Agrarian Japanese, the Ainu, and the Special-Status People." In *Making Majorities: Constituting the Nation in Japan, Korea, China, Malaysia, Fiji, Turkey, and the United States*, pp. 31–51. Ed. Dru C. Gladney. Stanford: Stanford University Press, 1998.

Oppitz, Michael, and Elizabeth Hsu, eds. *Naxi and Moso Ethnography*. Zürich: Völkerkundemuseum Zürich, 1998.

Pamuk, Orhan. *My Name is Red*. New York: Alfred A. Knopf, 2001.

Pratt, Mary Louise. *Imperial Eyes: Travel Writing and Transculturation*. New York: Routledge, 1992.

Prunner, Gernot. "The Ainu Scroll in the Museum of Ethnography, Hamburg." In *European Studies on Ainu Language and Culture*, pp. 229–268. Ed. Josef Kreiner. Munich: Indicium Verlag, 1993.

Rawski, Evelyn S. "A Historian's Approach to Chinese Death Ritual." In *Death Ritual in Late Imperial and Modern China*, pp. 20–34. Ed. James L. Watson and Evelyn S. Rawski. Berkeley: University of California Press, 1988.

———. "The Non-Han Peoples in Chinese History." *East Asian Library Journal* 10, no. 1 (Spring 2001): 197–222.

Revue des Bibliothèques. Paris, 1900.

Rhoads, Edward J. M. *Manchus & Han: Ethnic Relations and Political Power in*

Late Qing and Early Republican China, 1861–1928. Seattle: University of Washington Press, 2000.

Rogers, J. M. "Itineraries and Town Views in Ottoman Histories." In *Cartography in the Traditional Islamic and South Asian Societies*. Vol. 2, Book 1 of *The History of Cartography*, pp. 228–255. Eds. J. B. Harley and David Woodward. Chicago: University of Chicago Press, 1987.

Ruey Yih-fu, ed. *Fan miao hua ce (Sixteen Aboriginal Peoples of Kweichow Province in Pictures)*. Taipei: Academica Sinica, Institute of History and Philology, 1973.

Said, Edward. *Orientalism*. New York: Vintage Books, 1979.

Sasaki, Toshikazu. "On *Ainu-e*: Pictorial Descriptions of Ainu Life and Customs." In *European Studies on Ainu Language and Culture*, pp. 217–227. Ed. Josef Kreiner. Munich: Indicium Verlag, 1993.

———. "*Ainu-e*: A Historical Review." In *Ainu: Spirit of a Northern People*," pp. 79–85. Ed. William W. Fitzhugh and Chisato O. Dubreuil. Washington, D.C.: Arctic Studies Center, National Museum of Natural History, Smithsonian Institution; Seattle: University of Washington Press, 1999.

Schein, Louisa. "Gender and Internal Orientalism in China." *Modern China* 23, no. 1 (January 1997): 69–98.

———. *Minority Rules: The Miao and the Feminine in China's Cultural Politics*. Durham: Duke University Press, 2000.

Secret Palace Memorials of the Ch'ien Lung Period. Taipei: National Palace Museum, 1982.

Siddle, Richard. *Race, Resistance, and the Ainu of Japan*. New York: Routledge, 1996.

Smith, Kent C. "Ch'ing Policy and the Development of Southwest China: Aspects of Ortai's Governor-Generalship, 1726–31." Ph.D. diss., Yale University, 1970.

Società Geografica Italiana. *Carte di riso: Genti, paesaggi, colori dell'Estremo Oriente nelle collezioni della Società Geografica Italiana (Peoples, Landscapes, Colours in the Collections of the Italian Geographical Society)*. Rome: Società Geografica Italiana, 2001.

Song Guangyu, ed. *Huanan bianjiang minzu tulu*. Taipei: The National Central Library and the Institute for History and Philology, Academia Sinica, 1992.

Tapp, Nicholas, and Don Cohn. *The Tribal Peoples of Southwest China: Chinese Views of the Other Within*. Bangkok: White Lotus, 2003.

Teng, Emma Jinhua. *Taiwan's Imagined Geography: Chinese Colonial Travel Writing and Pictures, 1683–1895*. Harvard East Asian Monographs, Vol 230. Cambridge, Mass.: Harvard University Asia Center, 2004.

Thongchai Winichakul. *Siam Mapped: A History of the Geo-Body of the Nation*. Honolulu: University of Hawaii Press, 1994.

Tian Rucheng. *Yanjiao jiwen* (The Southern frontier: A record of things heard), 1560.

Topkapi à Versailles: Trésors de la Cour ottomane. Paris: Editions de la Réunion des musées nationaux, 1999.

Walker, Brett L. *The Conquest of Ainu Lands: Ecology and Culture in Japanese Expansion, 1590–1800.* Berkeley: University of California Press, 2001.

Watson, James L. "The Structure of Chinese Funerary Rites: Elementary Forms, Ritual Sequence, and the Primacy of Performance." In *Death Ritual in Late Imperial and Modern China*, pp. 3–19. Eds. James L. Watson and Evelyn S. Rawski. Berkeley: University of California Press, 1988.

Watson, James L., and Evelyn S. Rawski, eds. *Death Ritual in Late Imperial and Modern China.* Berkeley: University of California Press, 1988.

Wright, Daniel B. *The Promise of the Revolution: Stories of Fulfillment and Struggle in China's Hinterland.* Lanham, Md.: Rowman and Littlefield, 2003.

Yonemoto, Marcia. *Mapping Early Modern Japan: Space, Place, and Culture in the Tokugawa Period (1603–1868).* Berkeley: University of California Press, 2003.

Index

Page numbers referring to color plates appear in bold; those referring to reproduction of the Miao album appear in italics.